Ci*r*cle

Circle

The Ultimate Guide to Getting the Most Out of Life and Love

The Winner's Circle

Marion B.

Author

Copyright © 2014 by Marion B

All rights reserved. No part of this publication may be reproduced, distributed, or transmitted in any form or by any means, including photocopying, recording, or other electronic or mechanical methods, without the prior written permission of the publisher. For permission requests, write to the publisher, addressed "Attention: Permissions Coordinator," at the address below.

Socialization College Press
Ordering Information:
Quantity sales. Special discounts are available on quantity purchases by corporations, associations, and others. For details, contact the publisher at the address above.
Orders by U.S. trade bookstores and wholesalers.
www.instagram.com/AuthorMarionB
Printed in the United States of America

Publisher's Cataloging-in-Publication data
B., Marion.
Circle : The Ultimate Guide to Getting the Most Out of Life and Love The Winner's Circle / Marion B.
p. cm.
ISBN 978-0-69-228567-1
1. The main category of the book —History —Other category. 2. Another subject category —From one perspective. 3. More categories —And their modifiers. I. Johnson, Ben. II. Title.
HF0000.A0 A00 2010
299.000 00–dc22 2010999999
First Edition

14 13 12 11 10 / 10 9 8 7 6 5 4 3 2 1

Contents

Introduction xi

The Socialization Master
Talk and they will listen 1

    In The Beginning There Was Light 2

    Clear Your Mind 7

    Create Opportunity 9

    What Your Friends Said About Me 11

    Value, What Is Your Story? 13

    Is It In You 15

    The Test 19

    The Five Personality Traits 20

Mind Over Matter
Change your mind change your life 21

    Teach Yourself To Begin Your Journey 22

    Persuasion And You 23

    Hope, Why Winners Are Unstoppable 26

    How To Take The First Step 28

Contents

Why Are You Eating Two
Cupcakes? Because I lost
Ten Pounds!..30

If You Knew What Was Wrong,
You Would Not Have A Problem 31

The Emotions 34

What Is Jealousy?...................................35

Be The Change 37

Preparing Yourself 38

Be Positive..40

How To Catch Up? 41

Time Out 43

Groupthink And How It Ruined
Your Life 44

Concepts

Things to keep in mind 46

All I Have To Do Is Be Better
Than You, Easy 47

The 1% Is Overrated,
The 20% Run The World 49

We All Battle With Addiction,
Even Your Mother Gets High 54

Be Ready 56

Value And Television 58

Hesitate And You Procrastinate 60

Motivate Me 63

The Process 65

I Want To Do Big Things,
Where Do I Start?......................................67

Contradiction, Not What
You Expected?...69

Communication

You cannot unring your bell 72

I. *Body Language* 73

Soar To New Heights, Flyness..............74

Smile You Are On Your Way,
With An Appetizer.................................75

II. *Verbal Language* 77

Mirror Mirror On The Wall,
This Person Is Different 78

Communication 81

How To Be Social....................................83

Not Communicating
And What It Means 84

People

Know your audience..86

I. *What Is Really Going On* 87

Dream Mate...88

II. *Tread Carefully* 89

Emotional People...................................90

Bad Boy/Girl..93

Saying No 94

Contents

Physical Attraction

Doing your best 96

    The Attraction 97

    What Is Attraction? 98

    I Love Myself..99

    How To Lose Weight 100

    How To Workout..................................102

    How To Look 103

Talking To People

What people look for 105

    What Is It All About
And Why Is It Important? 106

    Emotional Contagion,
Your Happiness Is Contagious...........108

    Humor And Attraction 110

    Socializing, Baby Steps,
The Foundation.....................................112

    How To Appear A Little Smarter......113

    How To Be Famous 115

Talking To Your Potential Mate

Where you probably went wrong 117

    I. *The Tenets* 118

    Everyone Must Win 119

    Closed Mouths Never Get Fed 122

    Make Each Day Valentine's Day 124

    Masturbation...125

Contents

    Talking For Beginners……………………127

    How To Get People To Respond………129

    Meet A Potential Anyplace, Anytime 131

    How To Talk To A Potential……………133

    Why Some People Are Successful
While Others Fail Miserably……………134

    The Friend Zone…………………………135

    Networking………………………………137

II. *Approaching Potentials* ……………………………………………………139

    Is It True Love……………………………140

    Potentials At Work………………………141

    Potentials In Your Workplace…………142

    Potentials At College……………………143

    Young Potentials…………………………144

    Older Potentials…………………………146

    Approaching A Potential When
They Are With Other People……………148

    Approaching A Potential
On The Go…………………………………150

Dating

The good, the bad and the ugly …………………………………………………151

    Directions To Capulet's Orchard………152

    Dating Ideas………………………………154

    Conversation……………………………156

    Playlist……………………………………158

    How To Kiss………………………………159

    How To Dance……………………………160

Contents

How To Be Romantic 161
What To Cook 162
About Wine 163
How To Keep Them Coming Back ...164

Relationships
Keeping yourself and your mate happy 165

I. *Do* 166
    Investing 167
    Loyalty 171

II. *Don't* 172
    Just Getting Some Loving...................173
    When To Break Up? 174
    Cut Your Losses 175

Troubleshooting 177

Weight Loss For Women/Men...........178
I Am So Into Myself,
Why Do People Hate Me? 179
Controller..182
Moving On...184
How People Change 185
Live, Love and Laugh 189
REMINDERS 190
GLOSSARY..198

Introduction

Why do people cheat? Why do people buy things? Why do people change their mind? There is an 80/20 rule that states, the missing 20% is far more attractive than the 80% that people have. The 20% is the wow factor that some people possess and others lack. Communicate you are the 20% through body language, verbal discourse and appearance. The 20% is your smell, conversation, humor, positivity, capacity for experience, discipline, and your drive to socialize. All the things money cannot buy. This book shows you how to identify the 20% and use it to gain the advantage. The 20% you learn from this book will change your life. The difference is in the details.

Why this book? Science and experience separates this book from the others. We tell you the science behind why people do what they do. We coach and have experience solving relationship matters. Do you want a certain type of mate? Do you want to have a better life? If you want to learn how to get what you want, this book is for you.

You cannot continue to do things the old way and expect new things to happen. The old frameworks used to solve relationship issues do not work. There are reasons why things happen; we teach you how to change the why. Relationship counselors make an attempt to make couples agree to disagree. This is bad business, troubled couples have issues that require change, not

Introduction

concessions. Single sites are filled with people who are not exactly honest about themselves. Read what successful people are doing to attract mates and gain friends. "Circle," is a new spin on interpersonal communication.

Never forget why this book is successful! This book identifies what people need to add to accentuate themselves. The 20% people are looking for is contained within this book.

Want to know how people who are great in social settings keep others listening? Follow this book and your life will change. I have turned several school teachers into men and women who walk out the door with a mate each time. I have coached women who keep getting into relationships that end prematurely; I teach the women how to win.

We will show you how to keep people listening. Many people struggle with socializing, it is difficult and the digital world does not provide people with enough opportunities to sharpen their skills.

Once a person told me, if you want to hide something put it in a book. There will be many secrets revealed in this book; you have to read and follow the book to take advantage of the goods. The book is based on real common concerns that people worldwide have difficulties with. Reading this book will reveal the pieces you are missing from the interpersonal communication puzzle.

Who will benefit from this book? Many people cannot afford to pay a person on my team 5K+ to help them get a mate and friends. Alternatively, you can get similar training from our book. Follow the book; you can get and practice the same techniques my students use.

There is enough dread in everyone's life that all solutions become impossible and we settle. Your life does not have to be that way. You took the first step and purchased the book; you have demonstrated that your demands have changed. If the demand is great, you will work on getting the ability to change. If your ability increases, you will change. Remember, **you have to follow the book to get the results**. Want to get what you always wanted from life? Keep reading.

We searched through the piles of books available and could not find one that details how to improve your relationships with friends and your mate. The men and women that I have taught thought it would be a great idea to have a compilation of our teachings. They told me to write what we knew down and we did.

"Circle," will change the way you look at relationships with your friends and your significant other. What I know today was taught to me and I am passing it to YOU. I was just like you, I wanted it all and I knew there were some secrets to success.

There are better ways to do everything and communicating is no exception. How much do you know about body language and **Self-Disclosure**? Not much, we can help you. Inside you will find the resources that are required to get what you want out of life.

Information explaining why people have certain emotions will make you a winner. We refer to this information as, "**Knowledge of Self**." You must read this book to get Knowledge of Self. The book details why people have certain emotions and what can be done to elicit them. Once you begin to understand what makes you and others happy, you will become a "**Socialization Master**." Socialization Masters light up any environment they are in; they are special people who have Knowledge of Self.

If you understand why things work, you will be inclined to have things work for you. Beautiful things make people smile. Why do they smile, what is going on? Your body is wired and we will teach you how your body works. This book goes over the **Reward System** and why the others were wrong. This book shows the

Introduction

science behind why the other books did not work for you. You can inadvertently make a person feel bad if you do not understand communication. No one wants to feel bad. That is why the other books do not work; bad never equated to good.

Ever assemble something without reading the directions and find you missed a piece? Then you find most of your time was spent focusing on how things work together? "Knowledge of Self" is the directions to socializing. Here is where the line is drawn in the sand. The other books on meeting a dream mate and developing friends do not go over why certain things work. You are always left piecing the parts together. They never include the directions to socializing.

People follow the path of least resistance. The easy way is often a comfortable way. This book gives you everything you need to become a new you, without much work. Once you understand what is going on in a person's mind, you can start engaging them immediately. The book will detail the most efficient way to reach your goals. You will know what others have experienced and what they enjoy.

People love success stories, yet is that the only story? Did they wake up successful with a smile on their face? They probably had a smile, but we will get into that later. What about failure? Why do they always make winners appear as if they are not human just like you? Winners fail and they all have faults. They are just like you. All winners fail, the path to success is sloppy and filled with failures. Never feel ashamed to take a chance! You will fail before you succeed; failure is part of the journey.

Successful people fail again and again. On the exterior they appear lucky, they constantly try, once they win, the win is great since they always go for the big wins. What appears to be luck is the outcome of a series of failures.

Introduction

What about you? What should be going on in your mind? Start thinking as if you were successful. Remember, **the road to success requires you to appear bold; appear bold when you are not feeling bold.** Keep this in mind, if you are nervous, do not worry, the winners were also nervous. Remember, **keep going, the worst thing that can happen, will never happen.**

This book is not what you imagine it is; this is a guide to get you to the point where you are getting everything you want. Most will write this off as some book about getting a man or getting a woman. It can get you a mate and it can also get you across the Rubicon where you are your optimum self. This is a self-help book that reveals the real secrets, Knowledge of Self, **Starting** and **Positivity**.

We made a discovery while coaching people. We discovered, the people we coach were also living better lives and could brighten any room with their personality. We found their interpersonal skills were invaluable in all situations. Interpersonal skills are needed whenever you interact with any person. Calling this a book that only deals with getting a mate would only be half of the story.

The next time you look at a successful person, realize, you are probably looking at one of our students.

People who can get a mate are also great at communicating and communication is the most powerful weapon that we have in our arsenal. Would a country enter a war and not use their most powerful weapon? That would be foolish, countries are run by smart people and smart people never do foolish things. Talking is only one way to communicate; we also communicate with our actions. Body language is actually a part of communication that people are not familiar with. We talk about contradictions and how the verbal and body language must stay in sync. We show you what they are looking for. We are almost to the smile, keep going.

Introduction

If you ever wondered how a person can light up the room and wanted to be that person, this is the book for you. You have been given good advice before yet you probably were unable to decipher what is good and what is bad. Here is a rule that is reliable in every situation: negative advice and negative people should be avoided and passive people and passive advice should be avoided. Negative people are pessimistic. Passive people are not outgoing, okay with everything and do not stand for anything. Sounds simple enough, but do you avoid negativity and do you avoid the passive?

Listening and doing are two different things. Listening is passive, doing is active. Active people carry an energy that resonates and it is contagious. To boot, negativity and passiveness is also contagious. I could give you examples and it will get you going momentarily yet building on the idea will forever change your life. It is all **Dopamine**, I will sometimes refer to it as **Dope** and women or men who are high off of it will be called **Customers**.

Do not imagine this is some book about being nice and waiting for some person to give you what you have always dreamt about. You have to get out and get whatever you want. You will never find a hand from the sky giving you something because you are nice.

Who would want to be around a person who does not make them happy? That is Stockholm syndrome. Abusing a person mentally to make them want you is a foolish game. Many play this game and get poor results. Why would you want an abused person? They are not winning, you want to surround yourself with winners. This book teaches you how to win and make others around you winners.

This book requires action and change. Change is the only way to get to your goals. If you follow this book you will get the results you need.

Introduction

If you only follow what you want to follow, you will get mixed results. If you are told to do something and you do not do it, you will continue on your old path. You cannot **Build** without **Destroying**. If you just add on, you will have an addition. Additions never look as good as a new home. Build from the ground up. Do not let this book become another pile of knowledge, take action and give me feedback on the fantastic results you get.

https://www.instagram.com/AuthorMarionB

Bold items are located in the glossary. Have your highlighters ready; you do not want to miss a thing.

The Socialization Master
Talk and they will listen

In The Beginning There Was Light

Wow, they have it together. They brighten the room with their personality; they look good too. The opposite sex dreams about them. They always have something good to say and they are always having a good day. You know them. You have seen a Socialization Master (**Super**). They have Knowledge of Self.

You may have tried to imitate one of them. You imagined you had gotten it right. Afterwards, you watch as the Super reinvents their self right before your eyes.

Maybe it is the money, you get a new car but no one really notices you, only the friends who are usufructs. You change your wardrobe, buy the latest fashion and then you see them in sweats after a day at the gym. You watch as your neighbor's eyes glow while they are talking; they are in sweats! Finally, you get a new body, car, money and clothing yet your life is still the same. You are not happy and people do not treat you special.

What is wrong? You have met a Socialization Master. Their actions are deliberate, they know what to look for. They have Knowledge of Self. They do not just take action, they interact. The path they walk, is the path they have made a conscious decision to walk. They understand people. You can learn to understand people. You can reinvent yourself with a little help.

Is it something that they were born with? No, there is a science to social interactions. Many have tried to reinvent the wheel and failed; you cannot beat science. Many people rely on methods that are contrived and baseless. Those who light up the room have an understanding of the science behind the emotions.

Supers have advanced interpersonal skills. Forget lowering a person's value and other **Passive Aggressive** behavior. Actually, people want to be stimulated. People do not want their value lowered. No scientific evidence supports it, none. It is baseless, we have the real answers to the social dilemmas people are struggling with.

How do people interact with one another? There is a **Relational Self**, a person infers based on their present and past relationships. Decisions are made based on our introspective, our **Self-Concept**. If you are enthusiastic and bring a person up, they will want to be with you. When you are nice, a person is reminded of their friend and they will want to interact with you. Their interaction with you was inferred, it was based on how much your action resembled that of one of their friends.

There is a **Social Exchange**, a cost benefit analysis associated with a relationship. Look at what people are searching for; this will help you negotiate. Avoid incomplete people who cannot add to you. Remember, **Socialization Masters are complete people who only add to a setting; they are never in need and avoid those who are in need**.

There is a need to belong, people can be abused if their need to belong drives them to take **Affectional Actions**. Affectional Actions are actions that are driven by emotions; an example, you allow a person to hurt you because you imagine they love you. Love never hurt and it never will hurt. The need to belong is the need to be loved. Abusive people will use a person's need to belong against them; oftentimes, they will state, "No other person will love you like me."

In The Beginning There Was Light

There are coaches who teach students to use **Instrumental Actions**, people are seen as objects and manipulated to get a desired outcome. The approach is unethical and the effects are never long-lived. Socialization Masters use science to flow naturally and engage others. You will master interpersonal skills that can be applied to women and men. Gimmicky techniques will not get you far.

Now, the person who lights up the room, they will hereafter be referred to as a Socialization Master (Super). Their greatest trait, their Positivity. People release Dopamine when they are around them; they get people high off of their positive aura. They can mix it with sex if they are talking to a **Potential**, laughter and concern when around friends and confidence when they are conducting business. Positivity is the base they Build on.

Here is what we found on our journey. Successful women and men were interviewed. In addition, we closely watched their behavior. Many works written by psychologist were dissected. Once we gathered what we needed, patterns were identified. One of the two most startling findings, people did not realize what they were doing. They were accidentally charismatic. They made many mistakes; it did not matter. The second and last finding resolves why it did not matter. They were enchanting people, they were getting people giddy and the people appeared to be drunk. After some research, we found, people were addicted to their personality. Their body released something called Dopamine. There will be more on this. Keep reading, we will discuss this at length.

Why the high and low periods during conversations? The accident aspect of socializing. People do not realize they are hitting a sweet spot; they only do it for short periods of time. They also use comedy. Many forms of comedy are satires built on irony and sarcasm. Most funny people are very sad; full of highs and lows. They do not understand the power they wield. You can see women and men get high off of laughter. People love it.

You can also see people get high off of positive conversations; visit a church or a motivational speaker. Now that you understand, you can do it all the time. If you want to make a person addicted to you, get them high (Customer). The attractive person get them high, get the boss high and get your significant other high. Everyone can get high off of their Dopamine (Dope). Shortly, everyone you encounter will become a Customer.

You will become a Super. People will love you and many closed doors will open for you. Communication is very important. People have ended wars with communication. People have made money based on how well they communicate. The most influential people in history were great communicators. Martin Luther King Jr., JFK and Franklin Roosevelt moved people with their communication.

Did you ever see a nun spray graffiti on a wall? What if the female graffiti artist turned and told you she was a nun? She would need a little evidence to support her statement. The reason for your doubts, body language. Her actions contradicted what she was saying. When your look/actions contradict what you are saying, you will find people do not believe what you are saying.

Your body language is just as important as your spoken language when communicating. We will show you how to speak with your body and actions. A Super takes care of their body. You must also pay attention to what you look like while standing, sitting and speaking. Furthermore, your actions should be in line with what you are communicating. Do not say you are good to people and tip the waiter a dollar on a hundred dollar tab. You are always being watched and Supers understand this.

One of the most important things you must do, pay attention. You can be the person people are happy to see or you can be another face in the crowd. Always ask yourself, "Why am I impressed with this?" Observing your environment is paramount.

In The Beginning There Was Light

Supers get the most important concept in attraction: People never get what they want; they get what wants them. If you want someone, make certain you are doing things so that they will want you.

You will be a Super, you will master the art, pay attention and get Started

Clear Your Mind

Want to be the best you? We will begin Building, you will have Knowledge of Self. You have to follow the steps and you will be the new person you have dreamed of. What is it all about? When I was younger my snake died, I was crying and I was a sad little kid. My father asked me what was wrong and I told him. He asked, "What do you miss most about the snake?" He was **Breaking It Down**. All situations have to be broken down. Breaking It Down is defined as looking up the definitions to words to understand what is being communicated. You can then take a large problem and break it into smaller manageable problems. I told him, "It made me happy." He brought me a dog, I was happy again. It was the first time I experienced a person Breaking It Down. That taught me the emotion you get is more important than how you got it. An example, a man who wants an exotic car. You must ask, "What do you want to do with the car." He wants the car to get women and friends. The car is not important, friends and women are important, anything that will bring him friends and women will make him happy. That is an example of breaking a problem down. You want to find out what is the motivation behind a person's actions. You can also use the same concept on yourself to be the best you. Once you understand what you want, you can work toward it.

I cannot teach you how to become rich, but, I can get you the same beautiful partners that the wealthy have. I can get your friends to like you and treat you just as good as wealthy people are treated. Wealthy and beautiful people have the **Halo Effect**; you can get the Halo Effect without being rich or beautiful. You can have friends and Potential Mates (Potentials) pay attention when you speak and enjoy your company; you do not have to settle.

Let us be honest; men want money to get women. Women want a worthwhile mate. This book is the equivalent of a million dollars. You can make your problems disappear. We will teach you how to be your best.

How many times have you wondered, "What am I doing wrong?" More than likely you were focusing on becoming wealthy or waiting for your life to become perfect. We look at where we want to be and forget there are several avenues we can take. There is a science to getting what you want and surrounding yourself with beautiful people.

Communicating effectively and understanding how to break problems down will turn your life around. If you are happy with your current relationship with your mate, this book can show you how to strengthen that bond. If you are not happy with your current situation, the book will show you how to improve your life and relationships. If you are lonely or want people to genuinely like you, we have the answers. What you already know must be forgotten. You must clear your mind to begin your journey.

Create Opportunity

Heard of (your favorite company here)? There was a time when the company did not exist. There was a person who wanted to create something; that was it. The creators were ruthless; they had an idea and went with it. They did not know every detail, they only knew they wanted to create a company. The whole idea, opportunities are created. Great things do not appear; they are created and this book will teach you to create opportunity.

Why do we accept all the lies that are told to us each day? There is a great saying, it is the greatest lie ever told, "When opportunity knocks you better answer." When did opportunity start knocking? Do I live in a bad neighborhood? Opportunity never ever knocks. You have to create opportunity. You want a job, you look for it. You want to lose weight, you start exercising. You want a mate; you start talking to them.

We will show you how to prepare for life and create opportunities. You can get what you want with a little help. You must follow the advice in the book.

Do it, make a mistake, correct those mistakes and do it again. You cannot learn without taking action. Everyone has to find their niche. You only learn by practicing. Do not fall victim to the computer age, information overload. Information is useless. I had a friend who had camera equipment, she was learning how to become a photographer. Another friend called to use my camera;

Create Opportunity

he had a job taking wedding photographs. He did not have a camera; he tried and did a decent job. My friend with the camera and all the information never did as much as the guy with the boldness to take action. The person who barely knows what they are doing will learn more than a person who dreams about doing things. Do not fear mistakes; they are part of the learning process. Remember, **procrastinators only hurt themselves**. Create opportunity, no person will hold your hand and give you your dreams.

You must create opportunities to reach for your dreams.

What Your Friends Said About Me

A friend told me you make love to a person's mind before you make love to their body. If they feel high around you they will call you. Whenever they speak to you, they will get a laugh and some motivation. They will want to be around you even if they are not intimate with you. You can liken it to being around a beautiful person; you do not have to sleep with them and you will get pleasure from just being around them. The anticipation is what drives men and women. It is the thrill of the chase.

The anticipation, good memories and the hope is enough to get you excited. The anticipation is what make you high and turns you into a Customer, you feel good. You are releasing Dopamine when you are with them. They are addictive, whenever your mate makes you feel bad, bring yourself up by thinking about the person who made you release. If people are happy around you, they will want you around. You make them high. Once I asked, "Why do people feel comfortable enough to touch me?" I make them feel high and free, Customers. You will find that people will lose themselves and touch you because you make them feel as free as a child.

Make each moment memorable. Think of what is going on and would it be an If it will create a memory, do it. If you are hesitant to do something, too lazy to do it, that something is exactly what you should be doing. The average person does not have

What Your Friends Said About Me

Knowledge of Self; they allow their emotions and laziness to control them. People love doing the 20%; it is what memories are made of.

You can compare it to a lively person; they are positive, they make you feel good when they are around. They does not have to be the best looking person in the world. If they make you feel great, you want them around.

Remember, **keep it positive and make everyone around you laugh and smile**. You will become a "Socialization Master," once you have Knowledge of Self. The book will give you additional resources to Build on. You are always in one of two states, Building or Destroying. If you cannot figure out which state you are in, you are Destroying. If you cannot spot the boring person in the room, then you are probably the boring person.

You see how talkative they are, the laughing and the sophomoric body language, they are Customers. They are enjoying themselves. I made love to their minds. They had a great time; that is what your friends said about me.

Value, What Is Your Story?

How can I increase my value? Decisions are made based on value. Work on your story and you will become more valuable. You do not need the Ferrari or plastic surgery; you do need a plan.

You must first value yourself and stand for something. If you do not value yourself, how can others value you? Take care of your appearance. You have to look as if you value yourself by taking care of yourself. Remember, **if you do not APPEAR to value your look, others will not value it**. Have a presence and appear to take pride in yourself.

The book is filled with things to do to increase your value. Putting a person down will not increase your value, do not do it, it is silly. We go to New York and watch the other coaches. They have steps and lines to say to people, it is not natural and the results are poor. The best way to pick up anyone, engage them and stimulate their mind. When you engage you attract. When you attract you pull a person near because they are interested. A person can be interested in your knowledge, looks or personality. Use this information to edge the competition out. A potential mate who finds you interested will want to spend time with you. Give them a reason to call and they will stay in contact with you.

Think about this for a moment. People replay what happens to them in their minds and they also tell stories about what happened. What is their story of their interaction with you? If

Value, What Is Your Story?

you heard a story about your date, would it be exciting? Give people a story to tell another person about your date. Do not just go to a restaurant, go on a picnic. Do not go to the movies, go to a cheap play at a nearby university or city. Do memorable things that people will want to tell other people. Put your 20% into whatever you do.

Remember, **your story makes you valuable.** Keep reading.

What happened and can I get it back? "Lawyer," that was my answer. When I was a child, I knew exactly what I wanted to be. Life was that simple; I was confident and unstoppable. Parents guide their children and tell them, "Keep going, don't give up." They show the child what to look for. During your childhood, you are learning each day. Whatever you don't know, you can learn, children easily achieve their goals. Hunger fills your body and there are not enough hours in the day.

Your parents taught you what to look for. There is an awful fish story. Give a man a fish, he will starve, show him how to fish and he will eat forever. That is okay if you want fish and it works in that situation. What if there are no fish? Your parents did not show you how to fish, they taught you what to look for. This touches on **High Self-Monitoring**. They taught you to be observant, find solutions and be confident. They taught you to keep going and never give up.

One day we wake up and we lose it. Learning becomes a task, we become lazy and we settle. What happened, where is the hunger and most importantly, how do we get it back? Vanity, fear and **Groupthink** strike the child in you. You can turn things around, you can stop lying to yourself and you can live the life you dreamt about.

Is It In You

It is in you. However, you have buried the child in you. Children know what they want for Christmas and they know what they want to eat. Most people do not know what they want and they will accept anything that is decent. They will live anywhere, date any person and accept failure as the answer. Complacency has struck many; most are looking for a miracle to get them out of the hole they are in. Maybe they will hit the lottery, perhaps their partner will start to take care of themselves or one day you will get used to the poor life you are living. If you find yourself saying, "At least I am not doing as bad as them," you are in trouble.

You can win again, when people know better, they do better. Start thriving, you are already surviving and that is not too great.

Cut your losses! Do not continue to lose, you can die a loser if you do not change. It is in you, it does not require anything but a change of mind.

Now, getting yourself high and motivated. People only do things they are good at or imagine they would be good at. There are very few adventure seekers around. Keep the fact that there are very few bold people walking around in mind; you will be far ahead of the rest if you attempt something and fail. Remember, **a business owner who has failed is still a business owner; they have an experience that most will never have**.

There are very few bold individuals, you are actually playing a game where the odds are in your favor. If you stop your dream mate in the local coffee shop, you may be the only person who has stopped them this month. Beautiful people are feared, people imagine they are busy and they imagine they are taken. You may not get the first ten people you approach. Ultimately, you will be rewarded for your boldness. You will get what you want because you tried. Remember, **you have to go to war to enjoy the spoils**.

Did you ever look at a child and say every little thing makes them happy? What you witnessed was their Reward System releasing Dopamine. Each time we approach a goal, we release Dope. We get high when we anticipate reaching a goal. Your body releasing Dopamine is the surge you get before you watch an extraordinary movie or enter a party.

What is a Reward System and why is it important? A reward is used to influence behavior. A missing dog's owner may offer twenty dollars for the safe return of their pooch. They would not influence many people to quit their jobs and look for the dog. A wealthy owner who offers $100,000 would get people from other countries to join in on the search efforts.

The Reward System explains why you may or may not be successful while socializing. Our bodies releases Dope to influence us to do certain things. If we find ways to get the reward without working we will not do certain things. Drugs and pornography are examples of manipulating this system. If you do drugs, you will not be motivated to do things that naturally release Dope. Not surprisingly, a drug abuse sign, social withdrawal. No need to socialize if it does not make you feel as good as doing drugs. Pornography also eliminates the need to find a real mate.

Want to play with my toy? Children understand people must be coerced to experience new things. Adults forget a person must be lured into new experiences. Why would a person involve you in their life if they do not see an immediate benefit? Once a person is lured in, you can show them what a great person you are. Ask yourself, "What can I offer to get a person to see things my way." You have to give to receive.

What can be done about your current lack of happiness? How do you start releasing more Dope? It is very easy. Start setting small goals for yourself and you will become happier. Recall how you felt when you finished your last task. Repeat that feeling. We have small goals that we all have in common: the feeling you get when you get off of work, laying down in our bed, getting home and taking off your shoes. These are small goals that make you feel high. Remember how those goals felt? Set more goals and watch your happiness shoot to the moon. Each little thing you do will make you feel happy. Any little thing you do will make you happy. You will become as happy as . . . as a child. Once you start your childish lifestyle, you will be happier. See how easy that was. A little science goes a long way to prove, it is in you.

The Test

Ask yourself, "Could I have done that any easier?" If the answer is, "No," you are not working hard. If the answer is yes, you are trying a little and it is time for the next test. Could you have put additional energy into what you have just done? If the answer is, "No," you are on the right track. You have to pay the cost to be the boss, winners never give up and they work hard. If you do not have what you want, you need to work harder. If other people do not tell you, "You are great," you are not great. The good news, you can change all of this today. Go for your dreams and do not take no for an answer.

The test will always give you an accurate account of how hard you tried. If you could have not done it any easier, you are not trying hard.

Want a beach body? You find exercising difficult? Do you know how many miles that person with the beach body has jogged? They worked for their body and there was a time they looked just like you. You have to work hard. You have to pass the test.

The Five Personality Traits

There are five traits used in psychology. The traits will help you understand yourself and others. They are commonly referred to as the **OCEAN**, the characteristics measure how well a person floats in society. The OCEAN is comprised of Openness, Conscientiousness, Extraversion, Agreeableness and Neuroticism. Openness is a person's capacity for adventure and other experiences. Conscientiousness measures how much self-discipline a person has, not impulsive. Extraversion is the drive to socialize and stimulate others mentally. Agreeableness is the quality that prods people to be positive versus confrontational or negative. Neuroticism is the negative fiber that goads individuals to behave erratically and prefer negative emotions.

Neuroticism is directly linked to **Life Satisfaction**. Life Satisfaction is the way a person views their present and future life. A very Neurotic individual will view life negatively. Perspective can alter an individual's life more than any physical transformation or economic change. The finding accentuates why we coach our clients to view the world from a positive frame of reference.

Break your actions into these five traits. Positively display the four characteristics people find attractive and practice not being Neurotic. Never forget the five personality traits.

Mind Over Matter
Change your mind change your life

Teach Yourself To Begin Your Journey

What is one thing you can do now if you drop this book and do not read it? You can practice Starting. The most difficult idea in this book, Starting. You want to succeed? You want to strengthen your relationships with friends and your significant other? Practice Starting today! Starting is the most difficult part of your journey. Starting will put you in the driver's seat. The first question you must ask yourself each day, "How will I Start?" Put all of your resources into Starting. Starting will make you more powerful than ever. Anything that you want begins with you Starting.

How can a **Procrastinator** get the drive that an entrepreneur possesses? They have to Start the journey. Procrastinators will tell you, they never get Started; it is always difficult to Start. If a millionaire said, "You have to have 30 businesses fail before you become a millionaire," people would realize how important it is to Start the journey and failures are part of the successful journey.

Teach yourself to begin your journey. While you are procrastinating, a person out there is beginning a journey that will lead them to a beautiful marriage, beauty or money.

Who are you fooling? You lie to yourself more than you lie to anyone else. Your biggest lie, telling yourself you are okay and you are doing all that you can. There is no need to work until you pass out. However, you need to do more than the competition to get what you want. The hardest person to persuade, yourself. There are many people, maybe too many people who know things and they never use the knowledge. How many people do you know who know all about politics and never ran for office? People with talents who never made a penny off of their talent. Talent will not take you anywhere without Starting.

You will look your biggest enemy in the eye and tell them to stop holding you back. Your biggest enemy, you. Understand how you can persuade yourself. If you want to do anything, this chapter is for you.

Did you ever wonder why some people find it easy to do things while others fail miserably? If you are on the failing side, you probably fail at every task you have to do. You do not understand the framework of winners. There are several ways to skin a cat yet there is only one way to win. You must take action. You already knew that and that knowledge never took you to the **Winner's Circle**. It is time to put pressure on your target, you. It is not enough to know what to do, you must do it. This chapter goes into depth about persuading yourself.

Persuasion And You

People who can convince themselves to do things wake up each day with a natural high. Honestly, doing things turns you into a Customer, you read about Dope and you realize that if you try, you release Dope. If people get pleasure out of winning, more people should try to win. That is simply not the case. You have to get going to win and this is where people fail; they cannot get going. We have to first look at some winning traits.

A great deal of winners are entrepreneurs. What makes a person an entrepreneur? Many have opened small businesses. Most small businesses fail; the people who fail go back to their day jobs. Is this person an entrepreneur? Probably not. Look up the definition of an entrepreneur; that may fit the definition. However, they are not true entrepreneurs. The person with their own business has done something that an entrepreneur would do yet they do not possess the trait. More likely than not, the person opened a business doing something they are great at. The person failed and went back to working a nine to five. You may be thinking why would you open a business doing something you are not great at? You will more than likely fail, the world will end and everyone will laugh. This never happens, people celebrate brave people who act outside the box. True entrepreneurs realize failure is an integral part of success.

Getting up after a fall, that is the entrepreneur's trait. This is also the winner's trait. They get the job done; they do not care about failure. Their world never ends and they will laugh with you, they realize failure is a part of the success that brings you closer to your goal. Entrepreneurs fail many times, go bankrupt, get divorced and many take years to get to where they want to be. The entrepreneur understands you will fall; getting back up is what makes you a success.

Want to win? Throw yourself under the bus, ouch! Honestly, be honest. Okay, you need to lose to win, it may take time and I have to keep pushing myself. But how, how do you do it? What makes some keep going when others have given up? The first thing you must do is talk honestly with yourself. You may not realize where you are in life, I will help you clear things up. If you want something, you are not okay and you need to make changes to get where you need to be.

Doing a little goes a long way. Break what you need to do into smaller steps and you will find Starting is not that difficult. You will get to steps that are harder than others yet you are less likely to give up once you have put some time into your goal. Another thing to do, become a very positive person. The negativity is not going to get you to a point in life where you have everything.

What came first, smile or the money? Wondering why rich people are happy? It is not the money. You become rich by being a positive person and never giving up. Positive thinking is a motivator and you must practice it all day. Fake it until you make it. Look at positive things and the joy you get from them. Besides, you make others happy by being positive.

Want that new car? Want to go on vacation there? Some advertiser persuaded you; now it is time to persuade yourself. Next, we get into keeping yourself going.

Hope, Why Winners Are Unstoppable

Winners have a drive, it is almost arrogant. People wish they could possess the same drive. What is behind their drive and can you get it? Of course you can!

The driving force is hope. Once you win, you get high off of the Dope, you become a Customer. This feels great and it slowly starts to change the way you infer. This is very important, the way you infer is your perspective. It is mind conditioning. There are fears we are born with, e.g., fear of lions and tigers. Then there are conditioned fears we picked up. We know we were not born with the fear of robots. This is a conditioned fear; robots are evil. Television conditioned you to fear robots.

To infer is to conclude by drawing from specific cases. Specific cases, not imagined cases or vicarious cases. You make decisions based on your experience. Starting is the hurdle. Once you Start you can start to draw from your experience. Many ask, "What about your failures?" The body is beautiful, it does not release any happy chemicals when you fail and it can even make traumatic experiences difficult to recall.

Want to think like a winner? Hope is the driving force behind all winners. You will find your hope is more important than the truth. Use hope to keep yourself focused and grounded.

We all take losses differently. Some people lose and want others to lose or imagine everyone will ultimately lose. How do winners lose? They get back up and try again; they keep hoping. Getting up after a loss is very important, it starts the hope; hope gives you drive. Once you win, hope starts to push you. People make decisions based on their experiences and it is wired in your brain. Once you win, it starts to shape the way you imagine future outcomes will turn out. The brain's most magnificent trick, forgetting losses. Start to win today and program your mind to be hopeful. It is not a coincidence, successful people are brazen. Do a little digging and you will find successful people have their hand in many endeavors; they have realized hope is enough to make you a winner.

Once you get enough success under your belt, you will not recall your failures. Your perspective will change and you will become confident. You will have conditioned your mind to turn your fear into excitement.

Can you see confidence? Can you smell it in the air? You are on your way to confidence heaven. We have gone over the steps: Starting, losing and winning. Once you get a couple of wins you will notice how easy it becomes to do things that were once difficult. It takes 60-100 consecutive cycles to change the way you infer. We will call this the **Cycle Rule**. This is why Starting today is the best thing you can do. The sooner you Start, the sooner you can finish your 100 days. You will be alive 100 days from now, why not be alive doing what you want to do?

Building the drive that successful people have is simple. Work on your hope and immediately see a difference. You will be unstoppable once you build up your hope.

How To Take The First Step

Did you ever start a diet, quit smoking, or start eating better on Monday? We all have used the, "Monday line." Monday gives us an excuse to continue doing what we have been doing all along, procrastinating or as we all call it, handling **Cognitive Dissonance**.

Many people ask me or other people for advice. I will tell you a little secret, life is not that difficult. There are two types of problems; one you have control of and the other type is one you do not have control of. The problems that are beyond your control are health issues and other circumstances that could not have been prevented. The problems that are beyond your control account for five percent of your troubles. The good news, you can have what you want ninety-five percent of the time. All you have to do is Start.

Remember, **taking the first step is going to be a sloppy event.** No person has ever taken a graceful first step. The advice you get is probably accurate if the person giving it to you has done what you plan on doing. The little thing that they may have failed to mention, you will get to where you want to be but you will not get there gracefully.

Do not hesitate or talk yourself into believing that you do not want what you want. Losers are experts at telling you why they did not do something. Stay away from people who are experts at never doing anything. Find friends who are doing things and you will get some motivation. Take your first step, realize that you will fail. However, when you get to the Winner's Circle, you will realize, it was all worth it.

Why is Starting the biggest step? Humans are creatures who love habits. Look at people who are addicted to drugs and gambling; they are examples of how difficult it is to break a habit. If you start something and continue for a certain amount of time it becomes a habit. Create habits that will positively transform your life.

Take the first step and realize it will be a struggle before it becomes a habit.

Why Are You Eating Two Cupcakes?
Because I lost Ten Pounds!

There are many ways to motivate yourself and pleasure is one great one. The main thing wrong with most people, they do not understand how to manipulate themselves. We spend far too much time attempting to manipulate others. We work on a Reward System. If you reward yourself without competing you will not be able to motivate yourself. Rewards also make people lazy; it a bad idea to reward yourself prematurely.

When you reward yourself without working hard, you eliminate the "Need." Needs drive solutions. People create cures for things that exist. If there were no heart attacks, there would not be any cardiologist. Do not find a quick fix for your needs. Turn your needs into positive motivation.

Motivate yourself by giving yourself small rewards for small goals you set for yourself. Play games where there are rewards based on the game e.g., lose ten pounds and you can eat two cupcakes. A greater Knowledge of Self will change the way you do things and get you addicted to winning.

If You Knew What Was Wrong, You Would Not Have A Problem

How many of us do not know? Very few people do not know. The Internet has made everyone an expert in their own mind. A very important thing I tell all people, I only listen to actions. Knowing is not doing. Unfortunately, a common response from a person with a problem is, "I know" or "Here is the reason I am not doing what I need to do." Very few people with problems do not have egos that are out of control. Learning is a submissive venture.

Successfully convince me with your excuse; it will not change your situation. The only way to change is to change, listen and then take action. Do exactly what you are told to do and you will head in a new direction. Relinquish control and things will start to turn around. Knowing is never enough. Knowing is never enough. Knowing is never enough. Change requires action and assistance from a third party. People who listen to experts get things done; those who tackle issues alone spin their wheels. Large companies save time by hiring experts; you do not have enough resources to do it alone. Let an expert take you to your next level. We know the first step is taking action. Knowing is not enough. The moment you take action you will change.

Start working on your problems now. Speak with your actions.

SECRET CONTENT

What would a book be without secret content? There was a time when we listened to CDs. The very end of some CDs had a hidden secret track. The track would not be appear on the track listing. Similar to the CD, this chapter is not in the table of contents. Remember, if you want to hide something put it in a book. We understand, knowing is not enough. What is the missing piece to the puzzle? Skill is the secret. You must become Skilled. Having the Knowledge or saying, "I know," is not enough. You must be Skilled.

We shall **Break It Down**. Knowing means, "Holds in the mind." A person who knows has only done something in their mind. Knowing is useless. Now we break down Skill, "Competence gained through experience." People who are Skilled have experience doing a specific task. Knowledge is useless until is used to acquire a Skill.

Once you combine Knowledge with a Skill you have Understanding. Understanding is the highest level. We break down Understanding, "Knowing something thoroughly from a long experience." Once you have Knowledge and you are Skilled, you have Understanding.

You must be skilled and once you have a certain level of skill you will have Understanding. This is the missing secret that will transform procrastinators, those who are fearful and anyone who has a goal. This will take them to the Winner's Circle. The aforementioned people imagine additional information will help them solve their problem. They imagine knowledge will bring them Understanding. Being skilled is only way to have an Understanding. You must become skilled, knowledge is not enough.

The people who only read this book will walk away with Knowledge of Self. The people who practice and gain experience from what is in the book will have a Skill. The people who master their skill will have Understanding. This the only way to become a Socialization Master.

Getting a new skill requires work and dedication. A new skill is usually honed over a 100 days. This exposure is called conditioning. During their time which includes at least 100 cycles of doing what you are trying to accomplish, you must not break the momentum. First, an example of a person opening a furniture store and marketing the place. He must pass out flyers and market the store each day for 100 days. Next, an example of some person searching for a mate. They must approach someone each day for 100 days. If additional work is done on a day it does not count toward another day. Obesity, addiction and all problems can be solved using this method. Conditioning is used by the experts to modify behaviors. The next time you want anything you must go through conditioning to get it. Consider yourself skilled after cycle 100. If you are a carpenter you are skilled after your 100th contract. A blogger is skilled after their 100th post. Understanding is reached after your third year. An addict is only considered clean after their third year. Small businesses have a chance of surviving after the third year.

We will not discuss Skill again in this book. "Skill," is the bridge to Understanding and reaching any goal.

The Emotions

Angry all the time, fighting with people, domestic violence issues, sad or depressed? You do not have an understanding of how a person should think. You need some Knowledge of Self.

Emotional people can get themselves into trouble; they are led by their emotions. Your brain should guide you, not your heart. When the going gets tough, use your head; the tougher things become, the more you should think.

Emotions tell people it is okay to hit others if you are angry. Emotions tell people to drink away their pain. Emotions lead people down the path of no accountability. There has never been a time in anyone's life when anger or sadness has gotten them through a difficult time. Lose the negative emotions; you will become more productive and you will make better decisions.

Neurotic people do not like one another. Normal people dislike neurotic people. Do not act neurotic; you will scare people away. Neuroticism is the negative fiber that goads individuals to behave erratically and prefer negative emotions. Emotional individuals who complain and get angry turn heads because they are awkward. Do not act awkward or seek pity from people. The way to handle a problem, confront it and work your way through it. Negative emotions are a form of fear, people do not like people who are fearful. We like heroes, when was the last time you saw an emotional hero?

What Is Jealousy?

Jealousy is something that people who are jealous and people who are not jealous, handle poorly. Those who are jealous drive themselves crazy imagining crazy things. People who are not jealous are okay with everything; they let outsiders destroy their relationship.

Jealousy is an emotion and like all emotions except happiness, there is not one good thing that will come out of it. Again, negative emotions come from fear. If you fear, you are not where you need to be and you will be emotional.

You cannot passively control your emotions. You have to be cognizant of your motivations and stop yourself if you are reacting to an emotion.

Keep yourself relevant by reading my book and taking care of yourself. If you are keeping your money, mental, physical and sexual together, they will not want to go somewhere else. If they are driving you crazy, you need to go before you do something stupid.

Drop the emotions, start thinking and planning what to do. Never shoot from the hip, many get domestic violence charges or allow depression to take over their lives. All of this can be prevented if you just thought before you reacted. Once you have Knowledge of Self you will not be emotional.

What Is Jealousy?

You will get through the most difficult periods of your life without succumbing to your negative emotions. Remember, **never display negative emotions and never talk about your negative emotions.**

Jealousy is a negative reaction. Avoid negativity by using your head.

Are you stuck? Do you wish things were different? My neighbor went to an Ivy League university. When he went to school they made them forget everything they knew and go their way. Most people will never go to school there and who knows if they still do that at the school. The point, you must drop your ego to change.

What you are currently doing is not enough to get you where you need to be. You must listen to an expert. A mentor or positive example will help you get to where you need to be. Change is the only way to move from one level to the next. It is impossible to change if you keep doing the same thing. Insanity is doing the same thing again and again and expecting a different outcome.

If you want to learn how to ride a camel, ask a man who owns a camel. Talking to people who are where you want to be is a great way to start. Become a student, do what the teacher tells you to do. This is the only way to change. If you want to pick and choose what you should change, you will never fully change. Drop the ego and listen to good advice. Leveling the ground is first step to Building. Change and keep changing until you become fluid. Never get stuck where you cannot change.

Preparing Yourself

Could you look better? Do people tell you how nice you look? I don't care how you look! Do something for me. Look in a female or male magazine, look at all of the models, pick a look and go for it. I said go for it. Cut your hair that way, watch how they move, watch them speak, dress like them and most importantly carry the confidence they have. Remember, **if you want to hold onto anything in your past look and not change, put this book down. You do not have what it takes to become a Chief. Every Chief started out as a great Indian.** If you do not listen and learn, you will fail.

Should I use my new look on the people that I have had a crush on for years? No way! The people you chased in the past are in the past. You have to move forward, new people are easy and you may never see them again if you mess up. After some time as the new you, you can look at your past failures and revisit, if you wish.

A Potential Mate can cross your path anytime. I was on my way from the hospital when I met my current mate. If coming from a hospital did not slow me down, there is not anything that can slow a person down. Always know how to cut your hair, invest in your teeth and stay clean. Even if you work in the mud, you can look nice.

Did you know foreplay begins the moment you lay eyes on a person? Remember, **you sleep with the mind before you sleep with the body**. Unless you are very good looking, you have to be able to hold a conversation to get a mate.

Get rid of all the kiddie stuff. Hide the videogames and the doll collection. It is unattractive for a person to act as if they are a little child.

The idea is to be prepared. Socializing is a lifestyle that does not end. You have to love everyone and look great all the time. Prepare yourself, you never know when something or someone may cross your path.

Be Positive

Do you want to vent, let it all out and just have someone listen? You are driving some poor soul crazy. No one wants to hear that. There was so much traffic! It is raining and it is a gloomy day! Never say negative things; people are not excited about negative events. Remember, **only boring people get bored and only negative people have problems**. Only negative people see negativity. Take in some of the beauty in the world. Network and build some relationships.

Ever been chased by a person who you did not want to be with? Do not cut your ties with a person you do not want to associate with. Put them in the friend zone. Tell them, "I do not want to ruin our friendship.

Always keep a positive tone, it may get hard, ultimately, you will find it was worth it

How To Catch Up?

Catch up to what? Feel small in height, body parts, bank account, popularity, and anything you feel is holding you back. The word here is, "Feel." Most things people feel, other people do not notice.

The underlying idea here, leave whatever is bothering you behind unless it deals with cleanliness. Get clean and go for life. Do your hair, smile, wear a nice scent, exercise and speak about the pros not the cons.

What is the secret? The way you make people feel is far more important than how you feel about yourself. Most of my clients have money and are pretty good looking. They do not have the interpersonal skills to make people want them. My clients have what you imagine would put you into cruise control in life. Material things and beauty can get you attention, however, a great personality will keep their attention. Practice socializing and you will be more attractive than the person who you imagine has it all together. Make memories, have a presence and people will want to be around you.

People come to us after the nose jobs, steroids, breast implants and exotic cars fail them. I had to tell a male client who has a car that costs a little more than house, "You kill the dream when people enter your car and all you listen to is business news." One woman was so gorgeous everyone stared at her. Wherever she

How To Catch Up?

went she complained, she had a problem with everything. A great personality can go a long way if you know what to do.

Spice up your personality and your life will change. You will not only catch up, you will get ahead.

Time Out

Stop worrying, people who worry do not enjoy the present and their week flies by. A very close friend told me when first I started working, I focused on getting paid and enjoying my days off. I was told to enjoy the week and make plans during the week. I took the advice, my weeks started to slow. During the day, I complete small tasks and I walk or socialize each day.

You must stop to smell the roses. Seriously, stop and smell some roses. Pull over and walk through that park that you drive by on your way home each day.

Have a conversation and cut the television off. Television makes time fly. Take a walk with your mate or talk over some tea. Listen to music or play cards. Do not worry about everything. The most important gift is life and until you are laid to rest, enjoy every minute of life.

My mother would put me in time out when I went wild as a child. She just wanted to give me a moment to think things over. As an adult, I have noticed that we all need a time out, we need to enjoy what is going on in this beautiful world.

Groupthink And How It Ruined Your Life

Feel comfortable and powerful around your friends? They understand you? You are a Groupthink victim. You have found some other people in the world who support the weird things you do; that does not make you less weird. Yes men, yes women and yes friends are not healthy, they are poison. What is Groupthink you ask? The illusion that everything is okay since your peers are doing it.

Who can get affected by Groupthink? It has brought down companies, presidents, their cabinet and most people who are losing.

How do you avoid Groupthink and why is this important? You can avoid Groupthink by becoming as fluid as water. Take in knowledge from people who have money and power. You also need a diverse group of friends. The concept is paramount, the people you surround yourself with have the greatest influence on you; your surroundings become your reality and your baseline. An example, everyone in your circle is a little overweight. You imagine all people are chubby. You can be a few pounds overweight, lie to yourself and say, "Well I am not as big as my friend." You want to lose weight, spend time with people who exercise. Stay away from people who are doing worse than you. Remember, **there are times when we run from our fears by getting support from those who share the same fears.**

Groupthink also adds onto your confirmation bias. Confirmation bias, an idea that people can find something to confirm what they think, no matter how abstruse. Your close circle of friends share your ideas and will always see things your way. You need to have some friends who are different and have a view of life that can shed some light on your life.

When you are a leader of powerful people, you can ruin them, they will oftentimes go as far as doing things that are unethical or against the law. Remember, **always look for guidance from third parties who have no interest in your gains or losses**.

When you look up to a person, you are a follower in the group, be very careful. If you become the leader, would you have everything you want? Expand your horizons, look at real successful happy people, are you in that group? If you are not, you may be wasting your time.

Go to places where things are beautiful. Look at the people, homes and lifestyles. Do not emulate friends you have known your entire life. Read the story of any wealthy person, they have lived in many places and they compare themselves to great people, not average people. Be wary of groupthink.

Concepts
Things to keep in mind

All I Have To Do Is Be Better Than You, Easy

Turn off the television; you are not competing with movie stars. There is a great story about two men and a lion. The men are confronted by a lion and they imagine the lion is going to kill them. One man gets down and ties his shoes while the other man looks at him. The man who did not tie his shoes asks, "Why did you tie your shoes, the lion runs faster than us and it is going to kill us." The man with the tied shoes replies, "I do not have to run faster than the lion, I only have to run faster than you." The moral of the story: you do not need an exotic car, you only need to better than your competition.

Your 20% will set you apart. The tied shoes were the man's 20% in the lion story. Make your 20% set you apart from the crowd. Your story is what sets you apart. If you do not give people any memories, they will not have anything to talk about.

If you can release more Dope than your competition, you will become addictive and people will want to be around you. Exotic cars release Dope, if you can get one, get it and you can use that to get a mate and some friends. Most of us cannot get an exotic car, we can communicate and treat people better than our competition.

What does the dictionary tell us about intimacy? It says, "Close, familiar, warm and affectionate." You want to be intimate? Get closer, find common interest. Want to be warm? Listen and respond, you will be warm. Affectionate, check your ego, you do not have to be right all the time and empathize. Knowing how to communicate will level the playing field. When you feel the competition has outmatched you, remember, **it is just a feeling**.

There are people who make 100,000 a year, they get millionaires to invest with them. They convince people who run companies, who are very educated and who are very intelligent to believe in them. They invest millions. Knowing this, you should be able to get a partner who makes 50,000 a year to believe in you. Put it in perspective, look at value, you are not asking a millionaire out on a date.

Running faster than your competition is very easy. Pay close attention to the details and listen.

The 1% Is Overrated, The 20% Run The World

Has something caught your eye? It has caught the eye of others and it has had an influence on the brains around it. Remember, **the appearance of something is more important than the truth.** Whether the person admits it or not, it has elicited an emotion. People are constantly thinking and reacting to things around them. The wonderful thing about it, it does not take much to enter the minds of women or men. Remember, **you just need to showcase the 20%.**

If you are the one percent, you can drive up in a Lamborghini, that is wonderful and women and men will automatically love you. There are not many people with exotic cars. There are not many people with great smelling cologne/perfume. There are not many people who have an updated hairstyle. There are not many who have a positive outlook on life. There are not many who know how to make an inexpensive outfit look nice. Look closely at my last five sentences. Driving an exotic car is only one of five things that most people are not doing. You can stand out and you can have a presence without robbing a bank and buying an exotic car.

Ready to explore how you can join the 20%? We previously touched on being better than the competition, what does it really mean, what else is happening and how far do you have to go?

The 1% Is Overrated, The 20% Run The World

Well, it means communicating you are the 20% through body language, verbal discourse and appearance. Aside from making yourself happier, the people around you are happier. You do not have to become a motivational speaker yet smiling and communicating how great the world is helps. People remember memorable moments good or bad. People will remember how you handled a difficult situation. A difficult situation is an opportunity to lead. Remember, **if there is chaos or gloom, the leader will be remembered for their courage and ability to lead others toward happiness. Do not fall apart when you are really needed**.

Remember, **the 20% is the wow factor that some people possess and most lack.** Look at how great that dress looks, the little kid has manners and she is so positive. You have just been influenced by the 20%. The 20% you are missing makes others look whole. Just do a little more and the rewards will far outweigh the costs. The 20% is enough to get you hooked.

The 20% is what the competition is lacking. It can be communicated when it is picked up in a conversation while a person complains. Listen to what people complain about and make certain there is no person out there making that complaint about you. Communicate to people you have the 20% that they are looking for without appearing to boast. Realizing there is a 20% will get you far ahead of the others.

Communicate you are the 20% through body language, verbal discourse and appearance. The 20% is your smell, conversation, humor, positivity, capacity for experience, discipline, and your drive to socialize. You can learn to talk again, speak well, no complaining, no negativity and speak about where you are going versus where you are at. Additionally, make people feel good about themselves.

You are always communicating, pay attention to what you say and do; it could be taken the wrong way. An outburst will not be forgotten. Your actions shape what people think about you. Words can only take you so far. You can communicate you are a great person yet if you gossip badly about people who are down or scream at your children on the phone, people will not believe you are nice.

Your body language should be energetic yet calm. Look attentive but do not move too much. Stay in the front of the action and speak clearly. Look people in the eye and keep it positive. Have great posture and practice taking photos, be cognizant of how you appear to others. Whenever you see a great photo, ask yourself what makes this photo great? What about their body language is so appealing? Beauty is in the details; pay attention to details. I am constantly being educated on appearances whenever I meet people; there are so many styles that are used in a variety of settings. Remember, **always study people; study the actions of people in real settings, copy what is desirable and avoid what is negative.**

A thief's work is never done. Do you steal? I want you to start stealing the spotlight. Let others warm the place up; steal the spotlight once they drop the ball. Agree with positive things and play the hype person until something negative is said. Another gem on communicating. You can steal the center stage from a great host. A great way to steal a person's thunder is to wait until the person states something negative, downtrodden or in an envious tone, you reply with hope. Hope gets people going and it releases Dope. There are times when you can ride a person's wave and steal it from them when they veer off course. Remember, **most people who are good in social circles are doing it accidentally, they will make mistakes. You are conditioned and you can outshine any person; you are trained to pick up on their mistakes. Make a person's mistakes your strengths.** Remember **the lion, run faster than your competition and the lion will eat them.** This is the 20% they lack and you appear to have.

The 1% Is Overrated, The 20% Run The World

Did you ever say, that person went too far? You do not have to take it too far, just look at what the competition is doing and do a little more. A good way to do it, add 20% to everything you do. Always ask yourself, "Where is my 20%?" Whenever you get dressed do what you normally do and add 20%. Accessories and a good scent go a long way. The basics must be covered and add 20% to the equation.

Last but never least, what else is happening? When a person who has 20% enters a room, people notice and react to it. The person with the 20% makes the others say, I should have stepped it up a notch. You bring the competition down a peg, they now have to play catch up to keep the attention on them. You have made people notice you. If the competition has said something negative about you, they have made you popular and people want to know more about you. Good news or bad news, it is all news.

Look at how Positivity improves every situation. If you do 20% more, you will get some attention, do not go overboard. If you are positive, you can steal the spotlight from a person if they make a mistake. There are men and women who read my book who are not going to hit the singles scene and get another mate. They just want to be more attractive and this is how it is done. 20% and Positivity will make people like you. The last section covers the finishing touches on 20%.

Want people to love you? You can even make your enemies love you. Remember, **there is something that the most hateful person in the world loves, it is themselves.** Compliments work for people who are hateful and compliments work for people who are loving. Never forget the solution to a social dilemma? Cooperation, study how people cooperate. Remember, **people cooperate when they imagine they will benefit from the situation**. Who does not benefit from a compliment? I tell my sons to compliment people and they will take care of them. They are very small 3 and 5 yet they always tell people they look nice. They tell an adult they look nice, the adult feels great, in turn the adult treats them great and everyone wins. The adult will take extra care of them if I am not around.

Remember, **people like people who like them**. Whenever you are 20%ing around make certain you compliment people. When you compliment, talk about what you imagine they are interested in. If you see a woman who just came from the beauty parlor, compliment her hair. A man who looks as if he has hit the gym, tell him he looks great. You see a friend who is dieting, tell them they look as if they lost weight. You are probably thinking these things. Remember, **nothing is real until it is stated and acknowledged**. Compliment, it will keep the haters off your back and it will make your fans support you more.

Run the world, showcase your 20%.

We All Battle With Addiction, Even Your Mother Gets High

Back to Dope, you kept reading, first Dope then we will cover the smile in another section. Even Mom loves to smile, she is getting high and that is why she loves the kids so much. There is so much going on behind a smile. This is one of the most important sections of the book and it is the foundation of everything! Let us begin Building. Negativity and passiveness do not release Dopamine (Dope).

What is Dope and why is it important? Dopamine is a chemical that is released when we do reward based behaviors, motivation, and pleasure (laughing, sex and a winning), it makes people feel good. Dope is a free drug that I am selling to get mates, friends and make you contagious. Your body releases Dope when people do addictive drugs, during sex and laughter. The person who makes your mate laugh or feel good through positive talk is making them release Dope. They are getting high off of laughter and high off of positive conversation. Treatment for stimulant addiction is almost impossible; lack of the stimulant will create cravings and psychological withdrawal. If the cravings appear to be gone, it may rear its head once the stimulant is present again. A person is always chasing their high. People are always looking to feel great.

We will look at two reactions to a problem. A car cuts two cars off carrying two different couples. One car has the driver going crazy swearing and screaming. The woman gets in on it and they bring their Dope levels down. They later think about how stupid the drivers in New York drive. Meanwhile, the other car at the scene is carrying two Supers, the man goes crazy for one second but camouflages it with concern. It was no sweat, "Wow, that car almost hit us. We are so attractive, we even attract cars." The woman Super chimes in, "Or maybe that was an assassination attempt on the worst comedian in the world." They both laugh and release dopamine. They later think about how great their date is going. The other car with the low Dope complains and talks negatively for the remainder of the night, both go home and fall asleep. The couple in the car with the high Dope levels continue home and they have fun. The Dope filled car tells their friends the following day how much fun they had and how they cannot wait to go back out on another date. They are addicted to the stimulation; they want more and they are contagious. The couple looks back and pats themselves on the back. They kept their cool when it mattered most and they know most people are too weak to keep their cool under pressure. They know the near collision was a good show of how cool they are.

Listen to your mother, get high and get other people high off of Dope. Never let them see you sweat.

Be Ready

Always look good, look good at work, look good wherever you go and smell good too. A nice scent is the best thing you can do to communicate you are clean and it is okay to give you some love. Keep your mouth clean and exercise. Do little exercises before you shower and eat some food that can help you look your best.

Beauty is not what is seen on television. Look a bit more attractive than the people around you; this will take you a long way. Forget television, that beautiful person you just saw is sleeping with a person who has a normal job, normal car and a normal place. If someone notices you have style and grace that others do not have, they will be attracted to you. If you have a little clothing style and can keep a person laughing, they will want to spend time with you. Everyone loves smiling and people who are the life of the party have no problem picking up a mate. Want to see a Super in action? Watch the person at the party who keeps everyone entertained in a cool way; do not act like the goofy fool.

The key to looking youthful as you age, maintain your weight. A person who exercises always looks okay. Cigarettes also make people appear old, they loosen your skin and the sucking action ages the lips.

Fear is your greatest obstacle. Do not let fear paralyze you. When the opportunity to meet a Potential presents itself, take the

Be Ready

plunge. Remember, **getting the most out of life means sublimating your fear into motivation**.

If you see a beautiful person stop them, no person is going to knock on your door and say I am here. Be ready when you stop them, have a nice hairstyle and smell good. One or two nice pieces of clothing goes a long way. When you are talking, keep the eye contact going. Talk as if you have known them forever and make them smile.

Remember, **never forget that luck is when preparation meets opportunity**. If you are prepared and you get an opportunity, you will get lucky. The best thing about the formula, you can make your own opportunities by speaking. You can be ready by doing everything in this book. Mix the two together and you can get lucky.

Somebody will get lucky. If you are not ready and miss an opportunity, another person who is ready for the opportunity will get lucky.

Value And Television

100 dollars for a Rolex? 200 dollars for a Mercedes? Where is the value? Value has to be measured. You must know what is valuable and what is not. Those who fail, overvalue things that those with a Knowledge of Self do not value at all. Nice clothing is not valuable. A nice car is not valuable. Do not follow these things, they will not increase your net worth. They are not valuable. Television has made these items appear valuable.

Let us begin to break this down. People watch television and imagine it is real. There are many reality television shows, people imagine the shows are not contrived. When I was younger, there were a million alien and karate movies. There were people who would drink at bars and start karate fighting. There were also many people who called the police regularly with UFO sightings. People have been influenced by television since its inception.

Wow, they are beautiful on the outside. What do you do for a living? You watch what on TV? You dropped out of second grade? I can change you, none of that matters right, wrong! Most regulars at bars have issues. They are not the worst people in the world yet you will not hit the ground running with them. Stop it and think. Are you a bad person or do you keep dating bad people?

You can have value yet you do not act as if you are valuable. We look at what we see on television and imagine this is what others are doing. Television has a way of making the impossible seem mundane. People will not meet their future spouse in a club or bar.

You do not need breast implants or an exotic car to appear worthwhile. Albeit, you are expected to keep up with what America views as current. Additionally, people do not have to love you as you are. If you never exercise and do not appear to love your body, do not get offended when others do not love your body.

You have value and you can take what you currently have and make it better. Clean up your place where you live. Wear something very nice on Saturdays and Sundays. Take care of your skin, hair and teeth. Clean whatever car you have and fix your smile versus upgrading a vehicle. Whatever you have including your body and mind must be kept in pristine condition. You can be very valuable without becoming a television star.

Turn off the TV, it has made you feel as if you have low value.

Hesitate And You Procrastinate

Can't decide what to do? Someone else will make that decision for you. You relinquish control when you are in the middle. There is no middle. When you become tentative you are passing the keys to another driver. Another person is free to decide what direction you are going in. Things are always black and white. Gray does not exist. If you find yourself in the middle, you are not being honest with yourself. Playing the gray game is a procrastinator's game, do not play it; the procrastinator never wins, never.

Why so many procrastinators? What is going on in the mind of a procrastinator? The procrastinator imagines they are making a decision by not making a decision. The only thing that happens again and again is the decision is made by another person. Things are black and white. You should guide yourself and always decide. Making decisions has a positive impact on your body. Science has taught us the body releases Dope, the happy chemical, prior to receiving a reward. Procrastinators never position themselves to get a reward; they release less Dope and find themselves unhappy. They imagine life is complicated and full of failures.

A look into the life of a procrastinator will reveal something startling. They have failed very few times because they never do anything. A winner has failed many times yet the wins wash the fails away. Stop a moment and look at the life of Lincoln:

1818 Lincoln lost his Mother.

1832 Lincoln lost after running for the House of Representatives.

1833 Lincoln sold his failed general store share.

1835 Lincoln's girlfriend died of Typhoid fever.

1838 Lincoln lost bid for the Illinois House Speaker.

1849 Lincoln was denied a land officer position.

1854 Lincoln lost the race for the United States Senate.

1855 Lincoln loses bid for Illinois Senate.

1856 Lincoln was defeated in a run for nomination for Vice President.

1858 Lincoln was defeated in a run for United States Senate.

1860 Lincoln elected 16th president of the United States.

How many great losses have you had? It is unlikely that you have had one. Look at the life of a winner and you will understand that losing is part of winning. Always keep Lincoln in mind when you are searching for success. It took Lincoln over 40 years of great losses to become the president. What have you done? Now, we do not want to hear you complaining, Lincoln never complained, so you have no reason to complain. Start today, Start anything, just Start, NOW!

Fear will never help you solve a problem or help you win. Getting what you want out of life is why you should wake each morning.

Hesitate And You Procrastinate

What if Lincoln had hesitated? What if Lincoln entered a state of depression after his mother passed at such an early age? What if he procrastinated? The path of success has many turns that end in failure.

Never hesitate or procrastinate. You could miss a great opportunity.

Make every move a memorable one. I tell everyone to look their best at all times; it will make you feel good and motivate you. Treat yourself without breaking the bank. It is better to save a little more money and buy what makes you excited versus saving money by buying something less desirable. Make each day memorable and exciting. The only rules, make certain that the thing you are saving for does not take longer than 8 months to save for and buy it with cash, not credit.

A woman will be far happier with a bag that costs 1500 rather than a bag that costs 500. A man will prefer a television that costs 1500 versus a television that costs 500. The difference is worth more than the thousand dollars spent. It seems as if it not a big secret yet many people never treat themselves. If you buy an item because you saved some money, you will never look at it and feel good. Save for an item you want, each time you see the item, you will release Dope. Think of getting dressed up to go to an event. Remember how great you felt? If you feel so great, dress well all the time, you will feel better and people will compliment you.

When I was younger we played games and made innocent bets. The person with the highest score on a test won the money in the pool. Whoever scored highest on the state tests had their books carried home by the others. Play games like this with weight loss, dating or learning to speak another language. This will get you to your goal faster. Imagine if you are trying to lose weight and you eat a cookies after you have to run an additional 5 minutes. In a month's time you can add on an additional 60 minutes if you run three days a week. You may fail some days but you will progress more than a person who does not play the game.

Imagine a beautiful restaurant you went to. What was beautiful about it? Recreate it in your home. Was it the flowers? Buy some flowers, they are cheap. Was it the curtains, candles and white linens on the table? You can put these things in your home and live that way each night. Buy glasses, nice plates and silverware for your home. You will feel better when you eat. Surround yourself with beauty and you will lift your spirits.

Start winning and living better, you will be motivated.

Starting versus strategy versus outcome. Many people who we look up to were not born rich and did not look great in high school. They all made a decision to Start; they decided to change their life. Starting is the first step. They may appear lucky but they were prepared. Preparation is a strategy while luck is the outcome.

It is very difficult to have a great outcome with a poor strategy. The first step and most difficult thing you will do is Start. Starting is repeatedly doing something without a break for 60 to 100 days. This is referred to as the Cycle Rule. You will Start your strategy which is doing everything in this book including talking to 60 women/men on sixty different days and socializing. While you are preparing there will be several opportunities presented to you and you will become lucky. Luck is the outcome. When preparation meets opportunity, you become lucky. Luck is an outcome. The first step is Starting your strategy. There is a mix of preparation and field work. The final step is the outcome which is luck. You will become lucky once your preparation meets an opportunity.

You will not be at the beginning stage once you have approached 60 Potential Mates you have never met over a 60 day period. If you meet 10 in a day, it only counts as one. Do not skip any days. This technique can be used for weight loss, job searches and many other tasks people find difficult. We have to put time into whatever we desire. Any book that states you can use a few corny lines to pick up people is not worth the paper it is written on. Socializing requires an understanding of human behaviors and why people are perceived a certain way. Practice is also required to make new things become innate.

Again, you must follow this book with what we refer to as the "**Escape Focus**." If a lion were chasing you, how focused would you be on escaping? You would not leave your escape for later, you would not care what people thought of your escape and you certainly would not use the amount of money you have as an excuse to not escape. We want you to follow this book with that focus. Do as we say, do not skip anything, especially your look. Put that Lion on your tail and enjoy the process.

I Want To Do Big Things, Where Do I Start?

Want to motivate yourself? Focus on the 20%. In other words, if it does not make memories it will not motivate you or any other person. Overshoot your goals while taking baby steps and celebrating each baby step. An example could be weight loss. Sign up for a marathon. Another would be meeting people. Run for a public office, people love power and you will meet some influential people. Shoot for the stars, you will meet your goals and then some. You will probably lose the marathon and lose the election. You will however, meet many people in the process and lose weight.

Hate when all the wealthy people eat all the chocolate cake at the buffet? No, wealthy people rarely eat at buffets, they demand more, settling is not motivational. People who are not doing well are not motivated by their bad situation, they demand less. The lack of resources dissuades, it never persuades. People are not motivated to do things that they are not good at. We have seen through experience, the most effective way to motivate is by increasing a person's ability. Do great things to increase your ability if you do not have money or power. The greater the ability, the greater the demand. It is unlikely that a wealthy person will skip the line at the buffet, they just demand more than a buffet. Whenever you do something the average person will never do, you are motivating yourself.

I Want To Do Big Things, Where Do I Start?

Never want to do anything. Just do whatever you have to do. Start a countdown from four when you wake each morning. Do not lay there and struggle to get up. When you open your eyes, get up. On one you open your eyes, two you stretch and on three you are sitting up. When you say four, you have already been up. Use this countdown whenever you are hesitant about doing a task. This will be a mental cue to take action. You have already taken action by the time you reach three. The four is the first little win of the day. I tell my clients to start off the day by taking action.

Always do something you do not want to do before you do something you want to do. Do some sit-ups before you eat your morning muffin. People do not realize that winning will bring change. You will eat healthier once you start exercising. You will date a higher grade of people once you start hand picking potentials. You will be happier once you decide you will be positive. One thing begets another and it all starts with a decision. A decision to take action and shoot for the stars.

Start at the top, demand a little more and you will be rewarded for your enthusiasm with motivation.

Contradiction, Not What You Expected?

Have you ever seen a live duck? My son knows all of his colors and like most children, he loves animals. We take him to the petting park and point out the animals. I point to a duck and he says, "Where?" He tells me a duck is yellow. He then asks to see a yellow duck. I could not find one; he was under the impression that the duck was not a duck. The brown and black ducks were not what he had expected. They are yellow on TV. They were a contradiction. This is where the term **Duck** comes from. A Duck is a contradiction.

Lost your cool recently? A small mistake can have a great impact on the way people perceive you. Stress does not build character, it reveals it. The way you handle yourself under stress is your story. You can do the right thing 99% of the time. However, if your friends have seen you under stress and you are not in control, you may as well throw all those positive stories about you into the circular file. Playing it cool will always get you to where you need to be.

Adults also notice contradictions. People make an attempt to match what they have seen on television to real life. Remember, **people take the path of least resistance. They will not drum up a complex assessment of you. If you look crazy that is your story; no second chances.** You create a hurdle for yourself if you Duck around. This does not mean any little mistake will ruin

Contradiction, Not What You Expected?

your credibility. It does mean a big enough Duck will have you fighting an uphill battle to prove yourself. That was an example of an external contradiction. There are internal and external contradictions.

An internal contradiction is called Cognitive Dissonance. People love balanced predictable situations. When there is dissonance a person thinks one thing and does another. This is handled by avoiding/procrastinating anything that will remind them of the contradiction and hating/downplaying their desired result. We will go over two scenarios. A person wants a new car yet they cannot afford it at the time. The person will avoid going to the car dealer or talking about their goal of owning one. The person will also start to marginalize the importance of owning a new car, stating the cars are not as nice as some of the less expensive vehicles. The person sought to avoid thinking about owning the vehicle and also convinced themselves that new cars were not really worth owning. Losing weight is another example. A person will avoid going to the gym, weighing themselves and eating healthy food. The person will also state that most healthy people are superficial, ugly and have had plastic surgery.

Cognitive Dissonance is a sign of unhappiness. A person who has not worked toward their goals is not happy. They are settling. A person who is envious of others is not very happy. Do not contradict yourself. Do a little to work toward your goals each day. Do not have a contradiction on the inside or outside.

What can you do to combat external contradictions? Dress the part and practice good grooming habits even if you are not going to a wedding. People make judgments based on the information they have in front of them. Before you utter one word, you have been matched to a stereotype.

Would you let a well-dressed stranger with a Rolex borrow a dollar for coffee since he left his wallet at home? Probably, why, why do we automatically trust people who are well-dressed? It is

Contradiction, Not What You Expected?

the Halo Effect. A person's impression of you has an influence on how they treat you. Fortunately, you can influence a person with your appearance. Take advantage of the Halo Effect, do not let it work against you. The Halo effect is another example of why you should not do anything that would appear to be a contradiction.

When you contradict you settle. Never make concessions with yourself. Take action by starting. Look the part and act the part. If you are intelligent, live the lifestyle. If you are exercising, live the lifestyle. If you are good looking, live the lifestyle.

You actions and appearance define you. What is going on in your head does not define you. People will not speak about all the great ideas you have. They will only speak about how you have taken action and accomplished your goals.

Communication

You cannot unring your bell

I. *Body Language*

Soar To New Heights, Flyness

The reason you want to look fly all the time, people are always watching you. Keep it as fly as possible, at all times. **Fly** is aesthetically pleasing. Whenever you walk in a room look at everyone, if it is a social setting shake hands as you get to your destination. Do not walk into a room and not look at anyone you don't know, look at everyone as if you knew them. Looking at people conveys confidence. Be a social butterfly, you cannot win if you are shy, practice not being shy even when you are not looking for a mate or to impress. Look fly when you are doing everything. When you walk, walk fly, make certain you keep your head up and your posture is erect.

Look at yourself in a mirror. Do you look confident? Do not look too relaxed, it is a lazy look. Look at other people, what are they doing? Take the good from them, forget and avoid the bad. Look at yourself in the mirror do you look confident? Are you sitting up straight and are your feet on the floor?

You communicate with your presence more than you communicate with your mouth. Stay fly and act fly.

Smile You Are On Your Way, With An Appetizer

Okay smile, we will now talk about smiling and why these people who are overzealous get things done. This book will show you everything you need to know, however, before we begin, you will have to train your mind. Everything radiates outward. I have a friend who sells furniture. He was one of the first people who I had witnessed control every discourse. He could turn an unhappy person into a person who would smile and laugh. Of course, I asked him. He told me, "Communicate strongly, never give up communicating happiness and give people an appetizer to keep them happy until they get what they want." The appetizer is something to take the place of what they are complaining about. Do not acknowledge that you realized they were complaining.

He was also a smiling person. He always had a solution even when things appeared impossible. The smile kept him up where it was a far fall to unhappiness. He ignored negativity, when people started screaming, he looked as if they were speaking another language. If a person is upset, ignore it. Whenever a person came into his store screaming, he would smile at them and say, "Hey, how are you?" They would almost always complain about their furniture not being there on time, he would tell them it will be there tomorrow and offer them an appetizer (a lamp that he sells for $100 but he only paid $10 for). It would work like a charm, the people would calm down, get their appetizer and leave. He controlled the mood, he never let another person control the mood. If you are someplace and it is boring, it is your fault. If you are in a bad relationship it is your fault. People who are accountable for their actions and take action, get results. People with excuses spin their wheels.

Once you reply to an upset person, you make it real. Remember, **there are two worlds, the mind world and the real world**. Whatever people respond to is the real world and whatever they do not respond to, it is the mind world. Once a person responds, it becomes real. He would never respond to the screaming, he would just smile, keep himself happy and keep the person's screaming in their mind world. Use your voice and smile to make situations real. Furthermore, use it to change negative situations into positive ones. Keep smiling you are keeping yourself up and you are communicating you are in control. Do not allow a person to control the mood. Do not allow them to farce you to accept a negative mood. Remember, **a person can make you lose your cool or you can make them keep theirs**. Control the mood or have a person control it for you.

Remember, **the first thing to go before you blow your cool is your smile.**

II. *Verbal Language*

Mirror Mirror On The Wall, This Person Is Different

Want to fit in everywhere? If you find some people love you in certain circles yet you are not the life of the party in other circles, you are doing a poor job mirroring. People want to say they are not fake or accept me as I am. When you are around others, pay attention. Mirroring requires a bit of effort when you are around a new group.

Mirroring is important, it helps you blend in and influence others. People listen to people who are like them. If people find you have similar values, they will accept you and they are more likely to be persuaded by you.

Politicians are experts at mirroring. Politicians can find something in common with anyone. If they have not personally experienced what you are going through, they will tell you of a close friend who confides in them who has a similar issue.

Be creative, do not lie and learn to speak about details when telling stories.

Mirroring requires some boldness. You have to elbow your way into the conversation world; do not be afraid to join a conversation. Join a conversation that you see others of influence in. Do not join a conversation where the members are not influential. A very easy way to join a conversation is by agreeing with whatever is going on. Once you agree, you can also repeat something an influential person in that group has stated. Building rapport is easy. Remember, **if you get people to agree with you, you are getting them to listen to you**.

Do not forget to mirror tone and body language. Do not mock the group, however, pay attention to what is not going on and make certain you do not do anything that is not going on. People who are advanced can do other things to mirror, however, this requires an Understanding eye that most beginners do not have.

Watch how people running for elections behave; they are bold, confident and always share experiences that their audience has had. Politicians are great at interacting with people.

You do not have to turn on a television to see a great politician, in fact, the best politicians are at your City Council meetings and Board of Education meetings. Pay attention to people who appear to be in control; mimic their moves. I have a friend, he touches people on the shoulder. He is not a very large man. The little move breaks the space between people. Only a confident person touches people. He communicates he is confident by grabbing people by the shoulder. This little trick makes the most powerful and large men pay attention to what he is saying. The move is small yet it is the solution to a big problem many people struggle with, communicating confidence. There are other ways to communicate confidence, this is one that stands out above the others.

There are times when you can lead the circle the influential people are speaking in, shake hands with everyone in the room and make eye contact. There are people who may not have been there to witness your great parade of confidence. When you go over to the group, enter from the back and grab the leader's shoulder. They are immediately put on high alert. You have communicated you are confident and comfortable to invade the person's personal space. Only confident people are comfortable enough to invade a space that way. This is a powerful gem I picked up at a local city council meeting. Communicate your thoughts with actions. No one can see your mind; your thoughts do not count. Try the shoulder move and other moves that you have seen that communicate confidence. Never be rude, arrogant or belligerent while communicating. Rude, arrogant and belligerent people are not confident. They are just rude, arrogant and belligerent people that people do not enjoy. They are creepy.

Advanced people always find a common ground prior to approaching a person. You have to get rid of the creep factor before a person will trust you. Have something in common, get the person to agree with you, it is one of the best ways to get a person to listen and be open to persuasion.

Remember, **mirror or be creepy.**

Communication

You cannot unring your bell! You cannot erase what people have heard. You cannot be emotional, you cannot say something negative and take it back. What is so great about great speakers? They not only sell themselves, they motivate others. There are times when you will want to communicate effectively. Finding the definition to several wordy words will make you sound as if you are trying too hard. The missing part is detail. Whenever you use a word or phrase and forget people are paying attention to detail, you will sound ridiculous. You cannot talk at length about how the Romans built great structures and you have never been to Rome. Knowledge is useless if you do not get anything from it. A person will listen closely to a store owner and the same person will not pay any attention to a person who only read a book about how to operate a business.

You can read every book in the library yet if you live with your mother, you will appear unexperienced. Work on action instead of lip service. People will listen if you have some experience behind your words. Remember, **the best credential is experience**.

The digital revolution has made many experts. The bad thing about revolutions, there a casualties. Do not become a casualty, get real world experience and people will listen.

Want to learn what compelling speakers draw from? Speakers rely on the three modes of persuasion Ethos, Pathos and Logos.

Communication

Ethos is the experience aspect of persuasion that makes people believe in you. If a garbage man tells a person he is working with a doctor on curing the Ebola virus, people will believe him since he is working with a doctor. Pathos is the emotion aspect of persuasion that makes people believe in you. If a serial killer tells people he understands how horrible drunk driving is. He then states his mother was killed by a drunk driver. People will believe this guy since he has that emotional connection. Logos is the logic that supports it. If a CEO of a tech company on the brink of bankruptcy has better than expected earnings, he can back it up with sales figures. People will believe him if the numbers match the earnings.

Use the three modes of persuasion to communicate and persuade effectively.

Talk to everyone. If you are in a line, say something positive to whoever looks your way. Start a conversation with the person in front of you. Becoming a social butterfly requires you to be comfortable being uncomfortable. If you speak and a person does not respond, speak to another person. Getting there is not as smooth as you see in the movies, there will be rejection yet it is something you will have to get used to.

Get over yourself. No person is going to kill you, do not become embarrassed. The great thing about older people, they figured out no person cares. Do not wait until you are seventy to figure life out. Lose the ego today and you will find yourself winning.

If you are shy start off by saying hi to everyone you see. Next, ask every Potential you see, "Where is a great place to get pizza?" You have to become comfortable with getting rejected. Remember, **shyness is just a great fear of rejection**. The only way to beat shyness is to practice talking to people. The same way you were conditioned to be shy is the same way you can condition your mind to be bold. You will remember the people who have said yes more than the ones who say no. Get out there and speak, you will have a good time.

Not Communicating And What It Means

They are not speaking, what does this mean? People do not understand communication. The more you learn about communication, the more you will realize the words are not that important. Yes, people start revealing layers of their life to a Super who knows the revealing questions to ask. What? Words are not as important as what is being done with the words. Is the person passing time by speaking with you? Is the person revealing information that will bring you closer to them?

People who are talkative about any old subject are not in love with you. You are not forming any bonds with the people. However, if there is Self-Disclosure, you are gaining rapport and building a bond. There are two gauges of Self-Disclosure, how much are they telling you and how deep are they going. Beware, you must state your intentions or you will become a friend. If you are just a shoulder to cry on, you can quickly become another fool in the friend zone.

What is Self-Disclosure and what is friendly talk? How do I get there? Self-Disclosure starts with feelings about private matters. A person tells you a fact about something they would not publish in a newspaper, you are at first base and they imagine you are worthwhile (there is a chance they are just talkative, you are not there yet). Goals and aspirations, second base. Fears, dreams, emotions and complaints about their current or past relationships, third base. Attraction to you, sex or **Prognosticating** about trips with you, home run. A home run can only happen when people are in a relationship. Now, you get there by being enthusiastic, funny and building rapport.

Remember, **factual disclosures are less valuable than emotional disclosures**. Factual disclosure, "I am buying a house." Emotional disclosure, "I am so in love with the home, I borrowed money from my mother for the down payment." The aforementioned facts about disclosure and intimacy explain why people who listen are liked, they are able to elicit certain responses while people who constantly speak are viewed as arrogant and less trustworthy. You cannot get a person to reveal any layers if you are speaking. Ask questions, sit and watch as a person reveals themselves. When speaking ask personal questions, this is how people get into deep conversations. Be careful, one wrong move can throw you into the Creep pile.

Lack of communication at any stage is a bad sign. If you are dating and they are not communicating, they are bored or not into you. If you are in a relationship and they are not communicating they are bored, not into you or avoiding Self-Disclosure. They may be avoiding Self-Disclosure since they do not want to reveal how they feel about you.

Remember, **sharing is caring**. Remember, **if your mate or friend wants to talk, welcome it and it is a sign of intimacy**. The first thing my son does when he does anything or gets something, he states how he is going to tell his brother. They love each other and they share with the people they love.

If a person fails to communicate, you have failed to connect.

People

Know your audience

I. *What Is Really Going On*

Dream Mate

One percent of the people are super fly, drive exotic cars and are rich. Chances are, that dream mate that you are drooling over is going home to a person just like you. The first thing you have to do, only date people you would like to be with. You have to set the baseline high or you will end up with something you do not want.

You find nice people in nice places. If you live in a less desirable area, you may find a nice mate but they are looking for a person to bring them up and you will have a hard time building with the person. People who have things are looking for relationships, they will care less if you make 30K and are going to school. Go to a nice area and talk to some people there.

Outgoing people with careers are looking for a mate who will add to them. You do not have to be a superstar to get a mate who is going someplace.

Look past your surroundings for a mate.

II. *Tread Carefully*

Emotional People

Want to waste time on things that are not important? Do you like drama and people with out of control egos? You need to hang around emotional people.

Emotional people are bad news. Stay away. You cannot change them, do not attempt to change them. Temperaments are contagious, emotional people can bring the most seasoned happy person down.

A person with Knowledge of Self is conditioned yet they are not bulletproof. Stay away from negative environments. Persuading an emotional person to think about life rationally is a waste of time. If you cannot reason with a person, leave them alone. Normal people have a difficult time grasping the idea of people enjoying conflicts and drama. Some people like drama; it is exciting to some and it makes others feel important.

Why bad mouth emotional people? Spreading joy is the purpose of the book and we should try to make them spread joy, no? Here is the science behind emotional people and why an emotional person who decides to change themselves can change. The idea of a **Bounded Rationality** states we make satisfying decisions. People who make bad decisions are satisfied with their decisions. If you have additional ability, you will make different decisions. Decisions are not based on what is the most rational thing to do. People will always choose the most satisfying thing to do.

Decisions are also influenced by the amount of ability a person has. Increase your ability and you will make better decisions. If something is holding you back, change it.

We shall Break this down by looking at the definition of satisfy, ability and rational to further understand what makes people tick. Satisfy: to fulfill desires, to fulfil demands, give full contentment. Ability: competence because of a person's training. Rational: to use reason. We have to define reason since this is what rational is. Reason: to form conclusions based on facts. Now we understand what bounded rationality states about how we think. It is a person's rationale bounded not by reason but by ability and satisfaction.

People are making decisions which they are content with and fulfils their demands. These are in short, emotions. We all make decisions this way yet emotional people are further off their mark than the average person.

A person who is content with their demands will conclude based on that. People are making their decisions based on their ability, a person who does not have Knowledge of Self will not do any better since they do not know any better. Knowledge is part of your ability along with other resources at your disposal. The only way to modify this and have a person seek more knowledge, they must demand more.

Conclusion: unless a person demands more, they are content with their decisions. You cannot give them additional resources to make conclusions with if there is no demand.

Let us take the weight example. A man is overweight and he is satisfied for whatever reason. His wife asks him to lose weight, the demand is not that great and there are not any sanctions put in place. The doctor tells the man he should lose weight; he is at risk for diabetes. The demand is greater since his health is at risk and being sick will not keep him content. He loses the weight. His satisfaction with the situation had to change so that he could modify his diet. A comfortable person has no incentive/demand to change. Do not pay attention to what people say about wanting to change; look at their actions.

Behavior modification is always an uphill battle if the person is satisfied with their current situation.

The aforementioned explains why you cannot help a person until they want to help themselves.

Note: bounded rationality should not be confused with heuristics which is decision making based on experience. Heuristics does not factor in demands and contentment.

Bad Boy/Girl

Who does not want to have a little fun? Want to live on the wild side? Wild men/women can spice up your life. The stereotypes also suggests a wild person has a deviant love life. Again, turn the television off. You will have a headache that will not end until you sever ties with your wild mate.

Everyone is beautiful, everyone has good characteristics and everyone deserves a chance. However, if time is important to you, if you do not have a cape and you want to live a drama free life, here is some advice. People who have problems should be avoided. Certain people have bad luck their entire life. They are always in financial straits, they get into trouble and they always have arguments with people. These people should be avoided.

Bad luck is contagious, people with problems today will have a different set of problems a year from now. Ailments and getting hit by lightning just cannot be avoided. The other problems people have can be avoided. Their perspective is just negative. Look at their problems, if you had the same problems, you would handle them differently. Avoid these people. Surround yourself with people who do not have drama unless you are the drama type.

Saying No

Nice gal/guy, waiting for some loving to fall from the sky? Imagine the people you are going out of your way for will someday find you attractive? People will oftentimes take advantage of people who like them and will not get up the courage to say anything. The easiest way to say no, ask the person who keeps asking you for things out on a date. If they says no, drop them, you are eating your limited resources on a relationship going no place. If they says yes, it was worth it.

Having trouble saying no to a friend or family member? Tell them you are saving your money to get something, you do not want to but you have to say no. Sometimes you have to lie to avoid hurting people. You do not want to burn any bridges by being mean, just tell a little story about saving money.

You can also avoid people. I imagine if you are reading this you do not want to offend any person, so do not do it. There is one common thing about people that ask for stuff, they understand how to play with a person's ego. You are not important, after they ask you, they will ask the next person. They will get what they need somehow. Your ego has lead you to imagine you are so important and without you, they will just perish. That is not the case, you are just one option on a long list of people who will help them.

Saying No

There are times in a relationship when you have to say no. You are alive, when you show some difference. People will not hate you for standing for something. Remember, **if you do not stand for something, you will go for anything**.

Just say no.

Physical Attraction
Doing your best

The Attraction

You can do what every person does, be yourself and watch the odds stack against you or you can go out with plan. I prefer plans, some people do things accidentally and are partially successful. I am putting together a plan that all people can follow. You want to look and smell good all the time, a cheap scent beats no scent. Ask around, get whatever people have stated drives people wild.

Work on your look, make certain you are following the look of a model. It is difficult to get a perfect body yet you can work toward it while dressing like a star. This is what popular culture has stated is beautiful. Stay away from the look that singers, rappers and rockers wear. Some of their looks are too wild, dress like an actor or model. No gym attire, change your work attire once you get off and Woodstock is over. Also, get an updated hairstyle, go to the dentists and stand up straight. Look into the eyes when you talk and keep some mints to make your breath nice and fresh. Walk into a room as if you are walking into your kitchen, feel comfortable and look comfortable. Make eye contact when you speak. Talk to people as if you were talking to a child or friend. Do not appear scared.

Attraction, more than meets the eye.

What Is Attraction?

Why is that person attractive? The dictionary tells us attraction is a characteristic that provides pleasure or arouses interest. Do a little more and you stand out; do something mainstream, do not dress as if you are a vampire or a homeless hunter.

People who are pleasurable are attractive. Interesting people are attractive. People want to be around a person who makes them feel good. It is useful to forget what we think we know about attraction. It takes work and there is competition, people do not stop looking at you just because you are dating, married or old.

Attraction is something you can work at.

I Love Myself

Why can't I just stay like this? Why do I have to do this or that? I love myself. Loving yourself is a great place to start. If I change I will not be myself. You will always be yourself. You are not changing; you are improving. We bring our ideas to you to maximize what you have. You are adding onto what is already there. Do not act stubbornly, that is not attractive. Recall, openness from the personality traits.

Do you like nice things? Everyone else likes nice things too. Your appearance is your business card to the world. People make assumptions based on how you look, talk and your body language. Do your best to present yourself to the world as a normal person who has the 20% people love.

If you improve your look, you are still you. You will always be you, no matter how much you improve. Make everyone love you as much as you love yourself.

How To Lose Weight

Get a mirror and weigh yourself each day. Do not hide from yourself; you are on your way to a healthier lifestyle. Here is what I remember from chemistry class: it is easier to not eat something versus burning it off. A plain slice of pizza has 300 calories, cheeseburger 300 calories, rice 241 calories, small fry 130 calories and my favorite candy bar 280 calories. Now for the people who imagine you can still eat like a pig, exercise for 30 minutes and burn it off. The numbers: weightlifting 133 calories, aerobics 244 calories, yoga 178 and calisthenics 200. Eat a tiny cheeseburger with a tiny fry then drop down and do push-ups for 1hr and you will still not burn off those calories. Active people eat less since they are doing something aside from eating, they are burning some calories and they are doing instead of chewing. Joggers, a fast paced jog burns 10 calories a minute. That small cheeseburger and fry will take over 60 minutes to burn off.

A great way to start shedding pounds is to drink a glass of water before you order or prepare your meal. Water takes up space without the calories; most diets use water from heavy fruits and veggies to keep you full with less calories. The diet begins at the supermarket, who can stare at a bunch of cookies and not indulge? Stay away from the TV, a relaxed mind wanders and craves for comfort food. The experts state, "75% of overeating is caused by emotions," sad people eat while active people eat less. There is another positive thing about controlling your emotions

How To Lose Weight

If you find you are having difficulty losing weight, focus on your Conscientiousness. Conscientiousness is your self-discipline. Many people are not disciplined. Everything takes something and you have to give in order to take. It takes effort to lose weight. You have to give effort to lose weight.

Exercise at home, socialize and pick better foods. You will see the change.

How To Workout

You have heard it all before so why are you not doing it. Knowing what to do is useless, you must take action. Remember, **you have to do it to improve it.** Eat less and make little goals. Do simple exercises at your home. Exercise each day before you take a shower. Skipping days is for people who go to the gym more than an hour a day. Consistent exercise will get you into shape.

Running is also a great way to burn calories. You can meet a great mate running and doing other activities. Active people are usually of a higher caliber.

The diet starts at the grocery store. You cannot eat the cookies if you do not have them in the house. Buy children's snacks that are healthy instead of cookies and other garbage. Learn to love fruit and multi-grain bread. Eat heavy early. Your heaviest meal should be lunch. Eat a small dinner as soon as you get home from work. Keep at it, do not take a cheat day on the weekend and go until you see results. Exercise a little each day and do not take breaks.

You have to work to get results. There is not a piece of equipment out there that will perform magic. Magic is not the way to get into shape. Start small and keep at it.

How To Look

Has a stranger stopped you and commented on your clothing or hairstyle? Do people go crazy over the scent you wear each day? People want to be stimulated; stimulate them. Look like the people who the world already views as beautiful. The uphill battles are useless. Do not try to create your own style; follow what the stylist are doing to the stars. The look that you have had for the last ten years is not working. Pick three people from a magazine, copy their facial looks, hair and or style of glasses. If you are fat, try losing the weight. Weight makes people look older than they actually are.

If you are still not convinced your look is holding you back, kick your ego down a notch or two. Surprisingly, people with poor social skills have out of control egos. They refuse to conform to what society views as the norm. Update your look with what we are fed each day. Staying trendy is not a bad thing. There is something called the Halo Effect (HE). **This is a study that concluded most attractive people are viewed as reliable, smart, trustworthy and kind.** You can use the Halo Effect to your advantage; you can do a few basic things to improve your look. Studies have shown, people who are attractive are treated well. If you are a six on the one to ten scale, style your hair, lose a couple of pounds and smile. You can easily climb the scale with a few minor adjustments. A new look can easily take you up two points on the scale. People will treat you better. People who are warm, friendly and attractive get the most out of the HE. It sounds foolish and biased, it is better to know these things and use them to your advantage versus allowing them to be your downfall.

Look through the magazine and look at what the stars are wearing. Actors and models are the best to emulate. Go to a discount store and look for clothing similar to what they are wearing. I know some are saying discount store, not everyone can go into an anchor store and spend one thousand dollars. Discount stores carry decent discount clothing. If you know what the stars are wearing you can spot a nice shirt in a discount store.

If you hold on to something that you imagine is your style and do not follow the lead of the models, you will never get the attention you deserve. People are glued to popular culture. Give in and follow what the look is or keep looking cool to just yourself. I talk to numerous men and women who refuse to drop their bad look. Eventually, I ask a random stranger what could be done to improve their look. The stranger always tells them to do something similar to what is going on in fashion. Here is a wakeup call to those who refuse to change, remember, **keep dressing to make yourself happy, you will keep living and socializing alone**.

Looking clean communicates you are taking care of yourself and if a person sleeps with you, you will not stink or give them a disease. The disease issue is silly, however, people imagine beautiful HE people are even impervious to germs. The Halo Effect makes us imagine beauty equates to perfection. Dirty people look as if they have diseases. Both sexes want a good looking person. Want to spice up your life? Spice up yourself.

Let your old look go, it did not work and you did not get what you wanted with it. Peacocks are beautiful and they use their beautiful colors to attract mates; dress well, bring out the animal in them or someone else will.

You know how to look, now go do it.

Talking To People
What people look for

What Is It All About And Why Is It Important?

Do you have a close friend that you talk about certain things with? Why are you close? There are events and memories we share with others. Unfortunately, this all takes a great deal of time to establish. Fortunately, we know the secret to getting closer quicker.

What makes us close and how do we get closer? Intimacy, is what makes us close. This is defined as a physical and or emotional exchange between two people. The strongest intimate relationship is the emotional one. If people perceive a person as someone who they can build an intimate relationship with, they will gravitate towards them.

How do we get closer? The key is Self-Disclosure. Getting the other party to disclose information while reciprocating positively. The act of revealing one's self is Self-Disclosure. There are factual and emotional disclosures. Factual disclosures are things such as: I work here, I am married and I live in this town. This level of disclosure is not intimate at all; it is the crust.

There are two forms of emotional disclosure, we will call them the mantle and the core. The mantle is how the other party feels about things. These are facts that a person would not want others to know about: how they feel about others and thoughts on controversial topics. The deepest layer is the emotional layer, this layer makes a person vulnerable, and we can refer to it as the core.

What Is It All About And Why Is It Important?

The layer is comprised of: income, physical intimacy details and other facts that if revealed, would lower a person's value.

Self-Monitoring and getting close. Self-monitoring is understanding your audience and behaving accordingly. Again, the greatest communicators in the world are politicians. They are naturally High Self-Monitors or understand the importance of appearing as a High Self-Monitor. The term Self-Monitoring can be misleading, a High Self-Monitor is actually monitoring those around them, not themselves. A High Self-Monitor evaluates the surroundings and adapts to it. A **Low Self-Monitor** pays no attention to their surroundings and acts based on their emotions. Study your audience and understand what is acceptable and what is important. A High Self-Monitor can pick up what another person is feeling.

Becoming a High Self-Monitor will prepare you. When preparation meets opportunity, you will get lucky. There are times when there is an opportunity to get closer to a person, take the opportunity, it may never happen again. People who appear sad can be left alone or engaged. Always choose to engage. The question, "Are you okay," can break the ice and open a person up to disclose personal information. Such opportunities can save time that would have been spent building an intimate relationship.

Building an intimate relationship is not very difficult once you understand what makes us close.

Emotional Contagion, Your Happiness Is Contagious

Did you ever start clapping alone? Probably not, you clap when others clap. People mimic others and this is a very important thing to remember. Things are suggested and the crowd follows.

When I coach clients, they tell me how they want a girlfriend, boyfriend, husband or wife to find them irresistible. My reply, "Love everyone." They always say they are not as extroverted as me or how will it help them. People mimic others and the strongest personality sets the mood. Guess what is the most contagious thing you can do? Smile, people who smile at others get smiles in return. If you love everyone all day, they will feel great and you will feel great. People who make people feel good, are attractive and they are genuine. When you are out on a date, if you are good to your date while being mean or boring to the waiter, you contradict yourself. A good person is good more often than less. A mean or bored person is mean or bored more often than less. Great people are great to everyone, not just the people they are attracted to.

Emotional contagion is the idea that people will flow with their environment. People are on auto pilot; Socialization Masters are not on autopilot and understand the forces at work. Remember, **not making a decision translates into someone making it for you**. You set the mood, if you do nothing, the mood will be set by someone else.

Emotional Contagion, Your Happiness Is Contagious

Aside from controlling your mood, being the leader has additional benefits. Women who laugh more are more attractive. Happiness is contagious, laughing women make others feel good, this releases feel good chemicals in the body. Men who make people laugh receive telephone numbers at a rate three times higher than men who do not.

What makes this book different? We always go sit in on other coaches (we oftentimes get kicked out, I have to wear my 20% and I don't look as if I have a problem socializing). They tell the men in the room what they do or tell women what to say or do to attract men. The students then go out with these lines and come back with failure stories. The coach then tells the student well I said this and I was successful. Even the coaches who train others do not understand what they are doing. They never took the time to read about the science behind our emotions. You have to lead with your contagion. The line, "Let us get out of here," will not work if the person finds you boring and not likely to lead. The same line can be said by a person who is not viewed as boring and it will be a success. Remember, **understanding lines is not important, understanding minds is important, you can say anything if the person finds you contagious.**

90% of the coaches out there are good accidentally. You must understand the science behind the emotions. We took the time to dig through the tomes about interpersonal skills. Lines do not work, knowledge works!

Forget the horrible lines. The next time you see someone you are attracted to, say something positive, relative and funny about your setting. Your good emotions are contagious and you will get great responses back.

Humor And Attraction

People laugh and smile when they are having a great time? People cry when they are sad? People have a solemn look when they are bored or serious? Yes, yes and yes. You are now a body language expert, not quite. When a person is happy, you appear more attractive. The fastest way to a person's heart is through their funny bone.

When people laugh at other people, they are following. Leaders are attractive. Whenever there is a display of leadership the leader is attractive. People want to get as close to the leader as possible. There are many types of leaders, business owners, stars, funny people, intelligent people and attractive people.

There are very few instances when gender differences exist. This is one scenario where women must behave differently. Men who are funny are seen as leaders and people find them attractive. Women who laugh and appear to have a good time are seen as attractive.

Men who keep other men laughing appear outgoing and display leadership skills. They appear to be the most extraverted person around (recall, the E in OCEAN). A woman imagines she will laugh and have a great time with this man if they go on a date. The men who are laughing at the man's jokes are not seen as leaders. They have placed him in a leadership position by agreeing with him, he appears more intelligent and persuasive

Humor And Attraction

than the others. The leader has a better chance of going out on a date with the woman versus the men who follow him.

Now, the women who laughs versus the women who do not. The woman who laughs appears pleasant. She is also more attractive. A laughing women is more attractive and friendlier than a serious looking woman. The woman's laughing makes her appear as the most agreeable (recall, the A in OCEAN) woman around. The woman also fails to appear neurotic (recall, the N in OCEAN).

The science behind humor has differences, however, one thing is consistent, appear positive.

To sum it up, men act funny and women laugh and smile.

Socializing, Baby Steps, The Foundation

Start off by leaving your house and saying hi to 30 people. Once you do that, ask every person you see with red on, "Where is a good pizza parlor in the area?" Talk to everyone. Once you get the hang of that, go out with a friend and have them point out people for you to talk to. Start off with some small talk, then work your way into some more personal things such as: where are you from and would you like to go out to dinner with me some time?

Socializing also means, working a room. Whenever you enter a room, shake hands and talk to everyone you see. Introduce yourself to everyone and give each person you see a compliment: nice shoes, lovely earrings and nice colored shirt. People take time putting themselves together and showing appreciation is a great way to socialize. Make certain you wear a nice scent and you are clean. You can speak as if you are a Nobel Laureate yet if you have a Duck, you do not appear genuine. Do not contradict what you are trying to communicate. Keep the humor clean too, most importantly, keep it positive.

How To Appear A Little Smarter

People find others that have a degree or business very interesting. The obvious way to appear intelligent, go to school or you can make money. Having the appearance of an intellectual will not do much for you if you have no power. A very small business owner is looked at as being more intelligent than a person with a bachelor's degree that works a marginal job. The person who has a business has Knowledge and Understanding. You can do a little more than the average person and appear smart. Accomplish more and people will look at you as an intelligent person.

Communication can also set you apart from others. Communicating effectively requires that you look and act the part. You must appear clean, cut your hair nicely, wear neat form fitting clothing and do not appear animated while speaking. Do not speak loudly if others become belligerent, talk slowly and do not vary your pitch. Read and do not watch too much television. Learn about your community. Read and do things the average person will not do, it will put you ahead of the pack.

You can also participate. Experience equates to knowledge. If you are part of a decision making body, people will find you interesting. You can gain experience by becoming a member of a board or running for a local office.

The greatest thing you can do is create. Creating a business or creating a product to sell is one of the most interesting things a person can do. Anything you can do aside from sitting in front of a television will be viewed as interesting. A neighbor won the best garden award and she became a local celebrity. People always refer to her whenever they want additional information on gardening. Whatever you do, display your 20%.

How To Be Famous

You can become popular, this is very similar to becoming famous. You will get the same rewards. Make plenty of friends. If it is at work, you may want to keep it neutral when people start talking about other people. If it is at school, hang with different groups each day. Talk to your neighbors and go to local events.

You will have to do the **Work the Room Dance**. As soon as you come into the door, you talk and shake hands with everyone you see. Man or woman, give them a comment or notice something personal on them.

Women prefer comments about their hair, it is something they usually do themselves. If you cannot find a hair comment, talk about their clothes. Never ask where the item came from or how much it costs. Men love when people talk about their weight or clothing.

Small talk until you have met everyone. Do not spend too much time with any person, people like their time with friends. People also need an hour or so to become reacquainted with people they have not spoken with in some time; this is why you need to keep your introduction brief. Working the room is the most effective way to become popular without actually being popular.

Put your friendly face on wherever you go. People watch people and notice people who are friendly around others. If a person complains, do not start complaining, say something positive about what they complained about.

Famous people are popular and as you see, becoming popular is easy.

Talking To Your Potential Mate
Where you probably went wrong

I. *The Tenets*

Everyone Must Win

Ever seen a happy loser? You are asking a person to just give you their love or think you are a good person. You are telling a person you want to take from them; you want them to lose something. You are asking them to be a happy loser. You must first give them something and then they MAY reciprocate. Whenever you are looking to receive, start out by offering to give.

Money is not the way to go. Women expect men to have money just as men expect women to be attractive. A man with money or a woman who is beautiful is not necessarily a game changer, unless the man is wealthy or the woman is a model. A **Structural Approach** is the way to go. Once you understand why you should do something, it becomes a solution. If you are taught to eat when you get hungry, each time you get hungry, you will eat. The book illustrates how a Structural Solution can change a dilemma. You must show a woman or a man that you are not there to take from them, you are there to add to them. This approach will make others cooperate.

If both people are perceived as benefiting, the other party will cooperate. An example would be a woman who has just met a man, Jim, who wants to sleep with her. He could tell her how great she is and how he wants certain things from her. This does not benefit the woman, science has shown that it is very difficult to persuade if there is no benefit. He has communicated that he wants to take from her. She will more than likely turn him down.

Okay, the following is the same example, however, a Structural Approach is used to change the outcome. Suppose the man Jim, has a twin who has exactly the same life and he has read this book. He would indirectly communicate the benefits of being his woman. He will tell her about his future. He cannot wait to finish night school for welders. He will soon move into the gated development his friend and his wife has just moved into. Does she enjoy massages? He has been practicing a new watermelon and olive oil massage; it has been proven to relieve stress. The man has communicated he is a worthwhile catch. His current life does not reflect this yet he has foretold his bright future. People who are not where they want to be should start putting themselves into positions where they can ultimately become their ideal self. People who are able to Prognosticate, paint a better picture of themselves than people who cannot.

Women should also Prognosticate. An example would be a woman who is somewhat overweight. She can ignore her weight and tell the man how attractive he is. She can also tell him how he is very successful and he should take her out sometimes in his new car.

Now, let us look at her twin sister who has exactly the same life. She will tell him she is considering teaching at the gym where she has just lost twenty pounds. She can also mention she is moving toward her target weight twice as fast as the others in her exercise class. In six months she will begin looking for a house and she cannot wait until she closes. She cannot wait until she closes on her home so that she can get a new car. She is going to check her schedule and invite him over for dinner. She cooks a salmon that her family wants her to cook at every family gathering.

Remember, **when you are talking to a Potential you are negotiating.** People cooperate if they image they will benefit from

Everyone Must Win

the cooperation. Do not just tell a person how you will take from them. There has to be an exchange if you would like the negotiation to go successfully. This is a Structural Solution, very important to remember when negotiating. You may have known you should give in order to receive yet do you practice it?

Never forget, everyone must win.

Closed Mouths Never Get Fed

Fear is holding you back! Do you want a dream mate? Do you want to be happy? Do you want anything? Open your mouth! Things do not come to people, people go get things. The best Super can get turned down. Remember, **losing is part of winning**. Never fear rejection; it is part of the lifestyle. Always try, closed mouths never get anything. A "No" can get bounced into a date with some of the friends.

The fight or flight surge an animal gets when being attacked is the same energy humans possess. This type of reflex is very difficult to modify. The fear of talking to a Potential, making eye contact with others at a party or while walking through a room are conditioned fears. These fears can be removed from our system, this is called **Fear Extinction**. This is done through exposure. We are also animals. The distinction, we can condition ourselves to remove fears. Humans are too intelligent to allow our emotions to drive us. We can turn around and drive our emotions.

If you want a Potential tell them, don't make them your friend. If they says no, tell them to hook you up with some of their friends. Let them know you mean business. Okay, you do not like me so how about your friends, let us exchange numbers and you hook me up with one of your friends. Don't waste time in the friend zone. You need a friend, I will be your friend, look me up on Twitter. https://twitter.com/authormarionb

Closed Mouths Never Get Fed

You should be able to tell a Potential you want them. If you cannot tell them, get in a corner and tell yourself, you will survive and it is a number game, you must hear no before you hear yes. If they do not like you, go try another until you get one.

Boldness is rewarded, add some strategy and the best you. These are the ingredients to make a Super. You must try, closed mouths never get fed.

Make Each Day Valentine's Day

Forget Venus, her son is King! We all know Venus? She is the goddess of love. We see pictures of her; not much of a dresser. Venus and Mars have a son named Cupid. Cupid is the Valentine's Day icon. Many imagine Cupid plays only a minor role in love, as you will see, his role is a leading role. Anyone shot by his arrow is filled with desire.

In school we gave cards to the opposite sex on Valentine's Day. The cards communicated you liked the person. The children oftentimes became an item. Ultimately, this was stopped and everyone in class received a card, we do not want the children dating at such an early age. What was happening? Reciprocation, the act of rewarding a kind action.

Prodding is a way to encourage behavior. Cupid knew love needs a push. Studies show, people like people who like them. Telling a person you like them is enough to start the ball moving in the right direction. You are also encouraging them to like you. That is why you should always verbalize that you like a person. Just like, no love and no details. A simple like will encourage a person to like you. It is the science of reciprocity.

Do not come on too strong, a kind gesture is usually reciprocated. They may have never looked at you in that way yet they now have a decision to make.

Masturbation

Are you starving after you have eaten until you cannot eat anymore? Masturbating lowers your drive. People who masturbate do not chase the opposite sex. They do not desire their significant other and they will not go and look for a new mate. Several students greet me with zero drive. I ask, "When was the last time you masturbated?" They have all masturbated within the last 48 hours. There was a need to socialize and be merry. You can work on your socialization skills or you can masturbate. Why work on something if there is no need. If you eliminate the need, you will not seek a solution.

Incentive theory of motivation, what is that? You can liken it to feeding a woman who has just eaten a three course meal. When you are horny, there is a sexual desire. There is the incentive theory of motivation. The motivational phase. The motivational phase, darn masturbator. You eliminate the motivation that is naturally given to you when you masturbate. Science is speaking to you loud and clear. If you want to get a potential, you must stop masturbating. Limit your masturbating to three times a month. You will have more energy and appear more attractive.

Incentive theory of motivation, scientists compare your sex drive to hunger. The long and short of it: you will have an incentive to get a potential if you do not masturbate. Your body wants love even if you do not. Do not masturbate! The reason, there has to be a need in order to have a solution.

Want to feel alert and driven to talk and socialize? Do not masturbate. Masturbate on the 1st, 11th and 21st of each month only. Climax only 2 out of the three times, if you stop climaxing altogether your body will lose its desire. Your body will naturally release hormones that will engage you. Your body will release Dope if you anticipate getting sex. You will not get high off of Dope if you are already having sex with yourself.

Stop masturbating today, your life will change.

Talking For Beginners

Have you ever seen a person look uncomfortable? They are not full of energy and any person near them can see it. The same way a person can look uncomfortable, they can look confident. It comes from the mind and radiates outward. You must tell yourself, you deserve the best. When you see a Potential, tell yourself, this is the type of person I want to be with. It is no big deal, you deserve a great Potential. Talk to them just like you were speaking to your friend. The first few sentences you say must be assertive. You can talk high or low but you must talk as if you are comfortable talking to a friend.

People can see confidence. Look at yourself in the mirror and say, "What is your name? What do you look like?" Say it as if you are angry. Say it as if you are happy. Say it as if you are sad. Say it as if you have an exotic car outside and a person would be foolish to say, "No." The exotic car look is the look you should always have. Look at yourself, look at how the words do not matter, it is the body language that communicates, practice the body language.

Joke, ask questions, do not get too serious and ask outrageous question such as, "Have you ever been to Antarctica, I want to go?"

Keep eye contact and let the Potential know you are attracted to them, shy people become friends and bold people become lovers.

Try to make some plans to go out. If you are losing, keep trying. There are too many potentials out there looking for a mate, skip the ones that are not working with you. Make certain you are bold, boldness is rewarded in business and in life.

Every conversation will not end in you getting what you want. You will lose yet you will also win. If you make an effort to do something, a door will open for you. You just need ONE door to open to make all your hard work worthwhile.

How To Get People To Respond

Have you ever gotten pulled over by a police officer? Did he say excuse me, can I please have your license? He probably said, "License." He did not ask, he anticipated getting the paperwork from you. Talk as if you are going to get what you ask for.

Did you realize that? Your choice of words and tone can communicate whether you anticipate you will win or lose. People can see through words, that is why lines never work. It is not the line, it is the body language behind the line.

Work on yourself, everyone loves a star, it does not take much to be a star. Think of yourself, the person you are currently attracted to is not a star, they are just a little better looking than the average person. They are not rich, they are not close to perfect. They have the 20% you perceive as worthwhile. The truth is, television will make a person think less of themselves. They are not one of the stars on television yet you imagine you have to be a star to get them.

You are not competing against a movie star for their love; their current love is average. Do exactly what we have told you, look a little better than the average person. You are a television watcher yet you are still attracted to Potentials who are just a bit better looking than the average person. Do not forget the story of the person who was being chased by the lion, the person does not have to run faster than the lion. The person only has to run faster than the other person the lion is chasing. In other words you do not have to look better than a movie star. You just have to look better than your competition. Exercise, read, and look your best. It is all about being in a better position than your competition. It does not take much since most people come home and watch television after work.

You can get people to respond.

Meet A Potential Anyplace, Anytime

The last time my car had a flat tire, I was at the grocery store. I was not given a warning and I did not have another person with me to help. The point, anything can happen at any time so be prepared. I had a jack and a spare; I made it out of the grocery store parking lot in one piece. The same way a flat tire can present itself at any time and you must be prepared, a Potential can appear at any time and you must be prepared.

Keep yourself clean and presentable. Say hello to everyone, smile and keep some cheap scent on. Stop the Potential with a smile, if they keep moving say, "I just wanted a moment of your time." Some Potentials will not stop, they just don't want to be bothered. There are some Potentials who will not give anyone the time of day yet you must stop them and try. Try to stop them three times, then go on and try the next one. You may have to approach 100 Potentials before you get one that will work with you. That is okay since you will get one you like.

You have to keep trying, do not give up. If you are clean and you are ugly, it does not matter. Cleanliness is the most important thing, potentials want a person they can kiss and cuddle with. If your teeth are bad and you do not look clean, people will say, "That person looks dirty, I would not sleep with them." A clean ugly person with a great personality will get a potential if they try.

Meet A Potential Anyplace, Anytime

When you approach the potential, comment on their clothes or say their shoes are nice. Never ask if they have someone. Commenting and then starting a conversation is the best way to go. Most people can break the ice and start a conversation but they cannot connect. Connecting is telling a Potential you two should go out and grab a bite to eat. Just connect, if it sounds stupid it does not matter, practice it and practice it. A potential will respond and a response will show you what to do better next time. You have to take a chance and just ask to take them out. Some will say no to the best looking most experienced person, do not take it personal, you have to hear no to get to yes. The Potential that does say yes will make your day.

You can meet a potential anywhere, be prepared.

How To Talk To A Potential

Two things should be noted about Potentials, they are people and you should relax. Communicate you are attracted to them. Talk as if you were talking to a child if you find yourself getting nervous. Do not speak as if you are speaking down to them. Speaking as if you are talking to a child allows you to not take anything they say too seriously. This also allows you to be humorous and playful. Watch your tone, do not allow your voice to fluctuate too much. Body language can also communicate you are afraid or uncomfortable. Stand up straight and do not cover your hands. Eye contact is very important, look into their eyes, it is powerful and you want to communicate power.

Plan together, small plans are fine, this is what should be done with your Potential. Spending adult time together is the goal. Speak about where you two will go on the next date. Plan an hour in front of the tube watching their favorite flick. Tell them how horrible it was afterward even if it was good. Do not confuse this with putting a person down to increase your value. You are disagreeing to create conversation, never disagree to make a person feel bad. Playing devil's advocate will lead to more interesting conversations, boldness will get you into some interesting conversations." Talk about plans, ask questions and talk about them. Do not talk too much about yourself, talking about yourself is boring, if a person wants to know more about you, they will ask. Keep them laughing and sneak some touches in there.

Why Some People Are Successful While Others Fail Miserably

Do you like chocolate? I love chocolate and I have it at my home, I never turn it down when it is offered and it is a nice way to end the night. I like almonds but I am not that crazy about them. If I do not eat almonds for a month, I may not even think about one. One of the top reasons some people who seem normal fail with Potentials, they do not love Potentials. They are not Potential killers and they do not hate Potentials. Some people are just not into people since they have never had great interactions with people. They just want Potentials for sex or money. This is perfectly fine and a normal response at first.

Once a person improves their social skills, they will start to love Potentials. People fall in love with whatever they are good at. People who love people and Potentials have the greatest success. In order to get Potentials, you have to enjoy the company of the old ugly ones, the fat ones and the annoying ones. In short, you have to be able to get along with every person you see. A good way to Start is to speak to Potentials the playful way you speak to children. If a child bites you, or spits on you, you would not go crazy, it is a child, it is no big deal and it does not kill your ego. The child who bit you becomes a funny story you tell your friends. When a Potential turns you down treat it the same way, tell the story and laugh about it. You are on your way. You will be a success once you start loving everyone.

The Friend Zone

Wish they were more than just a friend? The first thing you have to do when you imagine you are in the friend zone, state your intentions. Your demeanor, also known as body language, will play an important role in communicating whenever a person is on the fence about you. Practice body language in the mirror. Also, look at how other people who you imagine are confident behave.

You have placed too much importance on what people are saying. You have become submissive. People are looking for a great leader and you have expressed you are just a follower. You cannot be the great leader they are looking for. When you talk to a child, you are leading the conversation, you do not take them too seriously, you joke, you ask how the child is progressing in whatever they are doing, you cut them short if they get long winded and you stay polite. You call a child a nickname and you are comfortable. You lead, lead the potential or the next person will.

Next thing you want to do is stop texting and talking on the phone. Meet the Potential someplace, hang out and talk around other people. Do not make any moves yet, hang out in a group to get the creep effect off of you. Most people in the friend zone are viewed as creeps (sorry to inform you nice people out there, people think you are creepy) so you have a little work to do before you can redeem yourself.

The Friend Zone

Take them somewhere where you can do some basic touching. Women will not have much of a problem yet guys have to make certain you are clean. If you did not try to replicate the look of one of the models in a magazine, you are way off. Your own unique style is creepy. Once you get some basic touching down, you can go for a kiss. You want to touch for an extended period of time. Holding a person while talking or holding hands while you two are speaking is a great sign. A good way to tell if a potential will kiss you back, go for a kiss (you thought there was some secret, if you fail, try again in 20 minutes). Basic touching is a great start and tickling is a definite sign. A person who laughs with you is interested, just go for a kiss. They are releasing Dope. People who make others feel good are contagious, people want to be around them. Keep it positive; you will not fail.

If you are scared then you just need to understand this is what women and men do. Start socializing more if you are frightened of Potentials. If you imagine that great looks, beautiful cars, money and prestige is needed, you watch too much television. I recommend not watching too much television, everyone else watches television and you can get updates from everyone else. Just socialize as much as possible. There are no Potentials at your home. Why are you home alone? Leave the house and get comfortable with people. Keep trying to kiss the Potential every thirty minutes. Never do it aggressively. Ladies will have better luck than the men. Men do not give up. Good luck.

Get out of the friend zone by being honest. I am interested in you, we can hang out next Friday if I am free. Never ask, tell, act assertive even when you are nervous. Exit the friend zone and live to tell about it.

Networking

Networking is an outstanding way to meet Potentials if you do not have an area such as a mall nearby. It is best to meet people through friends. Let people know you are looking for a mate. They would love to hook you up with one of their friends or family. One client used this approach, she landed a mate and a job for a friend within a two week period. They told me, "We were all successful following your, ask a friend for love, we decided to use it to land a job at a bank." Interpersonal skills work whenever you are looking for love, friends and work.

You should never flirt at work. You would not want to lose your job trying to hook up with a person. If there is an interesting person at your job, you can say, "Hey want to grab a bite to eat?" Do not push it, a "No" at work is the end of the conversation. Once you get them off of the premises, you can ask them to introduce you to some of their friends. Again, I do not suggest gambling with your job. Many people appear to flirt with people at work and act shocked when the other party reacts. I have seen many men lose their job because of sexual harassment. I have not seen a woman lose their job yet I imagine there are some cases.

You should be friendly everyplace you go. Whenever you go out and attend an event, enter and shake hands with every person you see. Talk to everyone, ask how people know one another, ask where they work, get as much information about your current

Networking

setting as possible. Once you find the Potential, talk to everyone around them, make certain they does not have a lover there. Separate them from the group and go for the information.

Networking is key. You must build as many bridges as possible. Never burn any bridges. When I met my current mate I was out with a person who owed me a great deal of money. If I would have burned our bridge because of the money they owed, I would

Remember, **if at first you do not succeed, ask about their friends.**

II. *Approaching Potentials*

Is It True Love

Do you think love will fall in your lap one day? No, you have to get going and find love. Remember when you were in class and you had to raise your hand to the get the teacher's attention? They were teaching you a thing or two about people. You had to take action and raise your hand quickly to get their attention. You must say the right things or they will move to the next person. Most Potentials do not know you exist. It is your job to find out if they are single and if they think you have the right answer. Only **Wounded Deer** shows overt interest in a person without the person doing anything. If you happen to see a person who likes you immediately and you are not a supermodel or Wall Street warrior, they are more than likely a Wounded Deer. These people are not a black eye on society but they may find everyone attractive. You may ask are you being viewed as a Wounded Deer? No, Wounded Deers are not doing their 20% and they are usually not very sophisticated.

Conversely, if you have stirred up some love connection by speaking to the Potential and showing interest, ask them to go to lunch with you. You must make it known that you are attracted to them when you go out. You must keep their attention or you are wasting their time.

Turn up the heat by communicating you are interested. You will find love.

Do you have a good reputation at work? People care what the people they work with think about them. You do not want the people at work to imagine you are a bad person. Other people also care about how their friends at work perceive them.

If they are at work, make certain you do not embarrass them in front of their peers. You may see a Potential who is interesting working at the mall or electric company. They may want to do something on the side but they have to act legit in front of their peers. Eye contact is King, this communicates interest. If you can get them to the side, do it and keep it short yet sweet. If you cannot get them alone, write a note, write a note, ask for their info, you can chat at a later date. Go for it.

The worst thing that can happen, your life stays exactly the same.

Potentials In Your Workplace

Do not talk to Potentials you work with, money is at stake. We went over networking at work which is a little dangerous. Getting a date at work is very dangerous. You can you're your job and damage your reputation. Flirtatious people at the workplace will get you fired, they are usually full of drama. Quiet people will get you fired, they are quiet for a reason. There are Potentials everywhere, do not risk your money. Get out more, take breaks, go to the mall, go to the grocery store and go to every family party a friend invites you to. If a person at your job is attractive, tell them to hook you up with some friends outside of work. You do not want to risk your job.

Once a person knows you, they can vouch for you. You can speak with their friends. The friends always look better. Networking will get you much further than you realize. That not so attractive colleague could have a knockout nephew or niece. Make friends with everyone, you never know who has that gorgeous relative or friend.

Potentials At College

Studying is the best way to pick up a Potential at school. You can meet to eat, try to make it off campus or somewhere where college people don't go. They may have a love interest on campus. If you communicate you need your privacy, they will understand since they may also be speaking to someone they are interested in.

You can also stop Potentials who are walking by. You don't immediately start trying to hook up. You can say, "Wow I really like those shoes where did you get them?" Always talk about their hair clothes or jewelry since people took time putting their stuff together. Silence is the worst thing you can do.

College love, can be a fleeting love. People are doing many things; do not put your heart into anything that may not be permanent.

Young Potentials

Young refers to a very attractive Potential who is more than ten years younger than you. Do not act as if you are getting the deal of your life. They can smell a sucker a mile away and they will test you. They know you are older and you just want to have fun with them. Stay away from any person under 21. Tell a potential you will call later and call days later. Always try to move a potential the minute you meet them, take them in the direction you are going or have a coffee nearby. Some of these people never answer their phones since they have someone. Call two days after you meet them during work hours. If they do not answer, text on the fourth day during work hours. If you do not get a response, try again a week later. If they have not responded after a week, give up.

Young people under 25 do not like being tied down. If they are very attractive, get in where you fit in. One thing about younger people, they are easy to get whenever you can get them, you must play the **Investing Game**. The Investing Game is simple, get them to do something for you. You have to get them to do something for you first. Remember, **people are chasing this person and they have a multitude of people willing to give them things; it is your job to get them to give to you**. You can have them make you lunch. Some of these things will anger them. Remember, **an angry person cares and you have made a mark.** Do not have them spend money. Money investing is only done while you are in a relationship. They can clean your place, make you food, fix a hole in your wall or wash your clothes.

People want to be needed and one way to separate yourself from the crowd is to have people invest in you. Just as the group of people who do things for them feel as if they are so important, they will feel the same because they will be doing things for you. This a great tactic to use on very attractive people.

The Investing Game makes people feel important. Albeit, it is called a game, people love to be needed. I have many clients who do everything for their significant other. This makes the other person feel as if they are a stranger. If you do not make a person feel wanted by receiving from them, they will go where they feel wanted. The person usually leaves and gets into a relationship where they can make a difference. When people invest, they care more about a person.

The art of investing its very powerful. We will go over this later.

Older Potentials

An older Potential is ten or more years older than you. Older Potentials are very easy to pick up but they are usually taken. Older Potentials are flattered you think they are attractive, pour on the compliments.

Older Potentials who are single are possible problems and should be thoroughly inspected. Remember, **do your due diligence, investigate your asset or it could turn into a liability.** If they are recently divorced or their significant other passed away, they are okay. If a person is 35 or older and no one has invested in them, there may be some underlying issue. People hide issues from people until their back is against the wall and they must show their albatross.

This not always the case yet decent people follow a pattern, one long relationship after another. This not the rule yet people who are single are usually single for a reason. A person who has just gotten out of a relationship or is in the process of leaving is domesticated. Single people can be unusually wild and you may find yourself trying to change a **War Hawk** into a **Dove**. Again, this not the rule but you need to know what dangers may await you. They can hide the fact that they are crazy until it is too late or you have time invested and want to try to work on things.

Older Potentials will let you know they are ready to mingle by laughing and being talkative. Once you see these things, go for it and ask to meet someplace out of town. Older Potentials will tell you what they want. If they tell you, they only want you for sex, that is as far as it will go. Do not try to meet their friends or family unless they want you to.

More than likely, an older Potential is just looking for fun and they do not want to be seen with you.

Approaching A Potential When They Are With Other People

Did you ever accept a person just because your friends accepted them? Peer pressure can work for you if you understand what is going on. A group is a unit and you must get the unit to accept you before you can take one of their members, if you are a beginner. Go to the point of resistance, it could be the complaining man in the group or the lady who appears to be having a bad time. Never go right to your target unless you are advanced. Going to the resistance point will get you in by having the resistance accept you or get you pity from the others since the resistance will treat you mean. Either way, keep going, talk to everyone and your target last.

Remember, **always ask the power question, "How do you all know each other?"** You can easily plot your next move once you know who is who in the group. Talk to everyone and make an attempt to get the target away from the group. You can leave to mingle for some time; the Work the Room Dance makes you more attractive and popular. If people see you talking to everyone they will wonder, "Who is that?" That will make you popular and more attractive. Furthermore, you will eliminate the creep stigma that strangers have. Go back around once you see your target separate from the others. You can go for it while everyone is not around. The best approach, separate a target; they will do things they would be embarrassed to do around their people.

Approaching A Potential When They Are With Other People

You can speak to a person you are interested in while they are out with others. You have to find out who is who and separate them from their friends. You can do it, people will walk with you to get a drink or walk outside for some fresh air.

A group must be worked from the outside in. You cannot just take people from their group unless you know what is going on first.

Approaching A Potential On The Go

Moving targets are always the hardest to hit. You have to give it a try and if it does not work, try again when another one passes.

Start off by getting close. If they are coming toward you and you are in a public place, you can ask for directions. Ask, "Where is a good place to eat?" If they are walking away or in another direction, get your speed walk going, do not give up, the worst thing that will happen, they say no and your life remains the same.

There are two types of Potentials, one who is open to talk and those who are not. If they will stop and give you a couple of words, you have an opportunity and the ball is in your court. Friendly people are always exploring. If they are friendly, they are checking to see what is out there. They are not necessarily promiscuous yet they love the attention or flattery. Some Potentials are looking for certain types and you just do not fit the bill. Keep trying, one will stop for you.

Dating

The good, the bad and the ugly

Directions To Capulet's Orchard

Romeo and Juliet, what a wonderful love story. Everything is perfect; this is not what you will encounter when searching for romance today. The process is sloppy and never plays out like television. You can meet people everywhere and I recommend common places versus bars and websites. The problem with bars and websites, some people are not exactly honest. There are good Potentials at the bar and online yet you have to sift through the crazy ones to find the good ones.

Sit at a Coffee Shop one afternoon and talk to people there. Go to a bookstore and talk to people there. Visit an anchor store and look for Potentials. The bar scene is full of undesirables, only talk to people at a bar if they are having a special night out or going out with their coworkers (read, Approaching A Potential When They Are With Other People). Stay away from people who know the bouncers and each person there. Apparently, they spend a great deal of time there and you cannot change that. If they spend a good deal of time at the bar, that is not changing anytime soon.

Always look your best when you leave your home. Go to common places, supermarkets, malls and book stores. People act more down to earth at a common place; they are less judgmental when you meet them at common place.

You increase your chances of success if you realize people are influenced by their surroundings. Studies have shown, men are less attractive after women have been shown pictures of male models. Women are less attractive after men are shown pictures of female models. If you are in a club and everyone is looking their best, good luck talking to the best looking person there. You also do not stand out as much when everyone is looking their best. If you are dressed well at the supermarket, you stand out more than being dressed well at a club or party. Recall the story of the lion chasing the two men; the man only has to run faster than the other man and not the lion since the lion will only eat one person. It is difficult for a common man to run faster than a group of lions. It can be done, why stress yourself out? Take your club outfit to a grocery store in a good town. Watch the people take notice, you can easily run faster than the average Joe/Joann Lion at the grocery store.

Dating Ideas

Suggest anywhere you can talk. Bring a bottle of wine and stop in a BYOB or park on the way. Try to keep the first two dates around people, they will feel comfortable and you can take them to a place more secluded on the third date. You can take them to your home on the first date yet you have to master body language and be advanced. Ask questions, talking about yourself is not interesting. Keep them laughing. As you grow and gain experience, you can do whatever you want. However, beginners need to play it safe. You are training, the experience you get from taking ten different people out on a date will make everything you do more natural.

What is said and the way you make a person feel during a date is far more important than taking them to the most expensive restaurant on the water. Keep in mind, you are being watched as you drive, while you are walking and while you are not looking. Your posture in a car or at the dinner table is more important than what you say.

Money is not necessary, women appreciate a hardworking man and men who are looking to advance. Beauty is not everything, men are looking for a woman who takes care of herself. If you are asked about yourself, communicate you are hardworking and you have plans to advance in the near future.

Keep them laughing and never act tentative in any way. Tell stories and make them funny. How do you tell funny stories? Talk about the details. Tell them how good you thought you were looking while you were wearing your favorite jacket and shoes and sat on a piece of gum. You imagined the waiter was looking at your shoes but he stopped to tell you about the gum that had gotten all over you.

Look clean, tell some funny stories, do not complain and show them you are attracted.

The best idea, make it memorable.

Conversation

Did you ever sit around silently and wonder what you should talk about? The best people to talk to are question asking people. What kind of questions do you ask? Ask questions about whatever they are interested in and ask questions about how they feel. You also must understand how to move the conversation. Do not sit and listen to stories about their last relationship or anything that would get them upset. If all else fails, ask about scenarios and what they would do in certain scenarios. Ask what they would buy if they had a windfall of a million dollars.

If they care about your life, they will ask you, do not talk at length about yourself and do not talk about things that make you appear smarter than they are. Keep it positive and never brag, if you are so great, people will already know.

Ask questions and they will be engaged as they ramble off about themselves. You can add brief comments about yourself as they speak but keep it very brief. Whenever a Potential is telling a story, stop them every so often and ask about details: was it night/day and how they were feeling when that happened. If they ask about you, keep it detailed and short, watch their body language. A turn away or gaze means you need to ask a question fast. Do not act as if you are a fan while you are asking questions. Question their decisions, this keeps you from looking like you are a fan of theirs. You are not trying to lower their value, you just want to augment or keep your value. Ask why they did not make a different decision or ask crazy questions that make them think a little. Keep eye contact at all times and never raise your voice.

Body language is very important. Supers keep an eye on a person's body language. They can tell if a person is happy, sad or lying. A person may say they are having a good time yet they are constantly on the phone and they are not talking. That person is not engaged and you are boring them to death. If this happens, get up and immediately take them some other place loud, crazy and cheap. The nearest bar will do; some people need action and you cannot change that. If they are still not engaged; take them home. You are wasting your time, they are preoccupied with something else and life is too short to play detective.

Cutting things short gives you time to do things that are going to give you a return on your investment. Only a fool wastes time.

Conversing is the key to becoming intimate. Read "What Is It All About And Why Is It Important" for detailed information about the levels and whys of communicating.

Playlist

Remember, you will win if you pay attention to detail. Music is an area where a connection can be made. Playing music a person is comfortable with will put them into a relaxed mode. If they hate your music, it may be a strike against you.

I prefer to ask, what type of music do you enjoy? Their choice of music could tell you about them. Look at the top ten songs of that genre and see what they like about it. If you have a woman who likes Spanish music and you play country western, you will bore her to death. If you are dating a man who loves rock and you play classical music, he will think you are boring. Do not assume too much; their choice of music is only an expression.

You are looking to get closer, give a little and make them feel comfortable by listening to their music.

The play in playlist means fun; make their listening experience fun for them.

Would a person think your look is clean? Check yourself: are you clean, do you look well enough to go on a job interview, is your dental hygiene in order and do you have gum or sugar free candy breath?

Look for signs such as laughing or make certain they are not uncomfortable when you touch them. Touch their ear or their hair. Look into their eyes and make certain your breath is fresh with something sweet or minty. Prepare your mind: relax, think about how good they look and squint your eyes. You two are having a good time and you both are attracted to each other. They have kissed before and they realize this is what people who like one another do. You are ready, make certain your lips are moist with a nice flavored lip moisturizer.

Remember, **you can influence the outcome if you have a great strategy.** Tell them how hot they look today. Slowly grab their face with both of your hands; their ear is between your thumb and pointer finger. Exhale away from them, begin kissing gently, inhale while you kiss, slowly tilt their head from side to side, play with their lower ear and neck. If you get pushed away without any hostility check yourself and do not apologize just giggle. If there is hostility prepare to slowly wind the date down, you are wasting your time.

Kissing is fun, if you are prepared.

How To Dance

Go along with it and practice in your spare time. If you do not know how to dance, bob back and forth. Let them do all the work, they probably just want have some fun. Look at videos of people dancing on the internet. Keep eye contact. You want to think sexy things while you are dancing. Look at the person sexy while you are dancing. Your body will start reflecting what you are thinking.

If you know how to dance, do not work up a sweat. The most important thing you do, dance if you are asked to dance. You have to be a social butterfly. Shyness is very unattractive. They just want to have fun and if you do not dance you are not fun.

You do not have to be the best dancer. Do not overdo it. Look confident when you are not confident.

How To Be Romantic

Romance is a lifestyle; it is done throughout the day. Most people will prefer a person who can take care of their needs in the bedroom and make them laugh versus a person who can write a romantic poem. You should translate the word romance into foreplay. You have to be romantic all day. Once the mind is stimulated, the body follows.

During the day, give your Potential a squeeze or kiss their neck. Offer a massage if they have had a hard day. Romance that we read about in novels is not what people are looking for.

Cook a meal or bring a bottle of wine but make certain you have your priorities in order. Bring a million bottles yet if you cannot make them laugh or act positive, you are not romantic. You have to love, laugh, and listen before you go and do these other things.

Romance is a lifestyle and it cannot be turned on when you want some love.

What To Cook

Cooking on a date is a great way to showcase how versatile you are. Make certain you are looking nice while you are cooking. Also, wear a nice scent and have some wine ready while the food is being cooked. Some small candles are cool and some flowers will make it intimate.

Spray some air freshener in the air before they come over. The food is not that important, some meat, vegetables, bread, and a ready-made bag of salad will do. Buy some desert, fruit or chocolate mousse.

Appearance is vital, it is the most important part of the date. People pay for appearances when they go out. The appearance of something is more important than the truth. A nice looking meal resonates more than a great tasting meal. A beautiful setting and average food is more pleasant than a date in a messy apartment eating some decent food.

Always stimulate the eye.

About Wine

Red with red meat and white with fish, chicken and seafood. Chile, Spain and Italy in that order, stay away from bottles from California. Do not forget to take the price tag off. Do not pay too much for a bottle and do not get a bottle that is very popular and cheap.

Wine is a great way to feel a buzz without getting drunk. A glass before a meal will make people ready to eat. Restaurants serve bottles of wine, add this to your budget and skip the appetizer and or dessert.

Hold the wine glass by the stem as if you were using the stem as a pen or pencil when you drink. Fancy stuff, also known as your 20%.

How To Keep Them Coming Back

Remember the television shows you watched as a kid? Can you recall when some of the shows used to end with a, "To be continued?" The show would give you a peek at the upcoming show. The show would end right as some person pulled a gun or as an actor received some news on the phone. The writers knew about Dope. They realized the brain would release Dope as the people who watched the show anticipated what would happen next.

When dating, we combine anticipation, the Cycle Rule and The Investing Game. When we do something enough times it becomes part of our life, Cycle Rule. When there is anticipation people release Dope. People who invest in things take care of their investment. Using the three, we can keep our mates coming back.

First we will use what we already should be doing, Positivity, appearance and Structural Solutions. Second we will keep the Potential coming back by making plans with them (Cycle Rule). The plans should include them cooking for you or them helping you do routine things such as spring cleaning (Investing Game). Last, we will always reward them with small favors, massages and small gifts (anticipation).

The goal, slowly make them a part of your life.

Relationships

Keeping yourself and your mate happy

I. *Do*

Investing

Tip the scales and you will do well. Later is here, Investing Game, the dirty secrets. They left you, they took all of their stuff you purchased and left. They left so easily, they, they and they. How can they just move on like that? I took them places, treated them well and brought whatever I could. I did everything and they still left. Ahh, you said it, you did everything. You did everything. You and only you did everything. What did they do? They did not invest so they left. They did not invest so they left. Remember, **they did not invest so they left.**

Experts, expect and equals all start with E and can give some insight into the future and help you see what is going on. Social Penetration Theory, hold on, it is not what you think it is. The theory explains investing. Relationships are intimate when there is Self-Disclosure and vulnerability. Self-Disclosure is a form of vulnerability yet we refer to it solely as the act of giving some person things that make you vulnerable.

Pay close attention: men, value your sex, if a woman is not respecting you, the last thing you want to do is to sleep with her. Women, your salary is not your value, if you are making less that does not make you less.

Back to vulnerability, giving a person a key to your place or car makes you vulnerable. Giving a person money makes you

Investing

vulnerable. State the importance of your gifts. If you do not give them any value, how can you expect others to give them value?

If you are invested in a relationship because of your Self-Disclosure and vulnerability and the other party is not, they are not intimate with you. You will eventually be disappointed since the other person does not have an investment in the relationship.

People who are not vulnerable are invulnerable. The definition of invulnerable is protected from danger, injury or loss. You are in a relationship where a person is protected from loss. You are capable of taking a loss while the other party is protected from taking a loss.

What is going on? If you are investing, you are putting in. If you have a stock, there are two actions you can take, you can invest or divest. To invest is to put in more, to divest is to take. If you are constantly investing in a relationship the other is divesting. Procrastinators will say they are taking action by not making a decision, things are at a standstill. If you do not make a decision, one will be made for you. Remember, **if a person is not giving they are taking**.

Everyone has something to invest. If they do not invest in you, they are investing in themselves. When people invest, they take care of their investment. People never destroy what they have invested in.

They had zero attachments, no skin in the game, no dog in the fight and my personal favorite, nothing to lose. People take care of their investment. If a person buys something, they take care of it more than they take care of something they did not buy. If a person goes out of the way to help another person, they care about their well-being. People also pay attention to what they invest in.

Whenever a person has to put their resources into something, they are more frugal. An example would be an open bar. The average

Investing

person may go and have a drink or two, however, when there is an open bar, people go crazy. People who do not drink regularly get drunk and the drinkers go wild. There is not an investment, just a free ride that people always take advantage of. If you do not get your mate to invest, you are the open bar in the relationship; they are happy as long as the free drinks keep coming.

There are parties where people are asked to bring a dish. These are the parties where people are congratulated for their great dish. Everyone in attendance had to put in energy to make a dish. The dish exchange makes people humble, they realize what it takes to make a dish. Remember, **you want your relationship to be the party where everyone brings a dish.**

When you are the open bar in the relationship, your mate has no attachments. They will not appreciate what you do for them since they do not do anything for you. They do not understand the sacrifices that are made if they do not sacrifice. You cannot have a lazy person without an enabler. If your mate is not contributing, pat yourself on the back, you are an enabler.

When I was a kid, I brought my mother a Mother's Day card. One day my mother threw out the card, I asked her why did she throw it out? She told me she threw out the cards my father and brother had given her a month ago and kept my card longer since she liked the lady's dress on it. I did not notice she had thrown the others away some time ago. I only noticed what I had given her. Even children only pay attention to what they invest in.

When a significant other does not have an investment in the relationship, they do not have any reason to stay when a problem arises.

Man files for a divorce and the woman jumps out the window. Why did the woman jump out the window? The woman had more invested in the relationship and was destroyed when she

Investing

heard her investment tanked. If the man had more of an investment in the relationship, they would have looked at working on the relationship.

Investing does not mean just money, people can also invest time and people can invest energy. Before we get into investing, we must go over the social dilemma. How do both parties walk away with a Dope high? How can someone do something for another person and feel good? Let us imagine you ask your partner to make you a widget. One thing you are doing when you ask (not force or order) a person to do something is putting yourself into a harmless submissive position. You are making another person superior without taking any orders. You both are winning. You are getting something from a person and the other party is in control since they are needed. You are making a person feel needed.

When you ask for things you are getting people to invest; without an investment the other person has nothing to lose.

Loyalty

Innocence is the honeymoon phase. Keeping a relationship in the honeymoon phase is relatively simple. Stay loyal, do not lie and treat your mate as if they were your favorite exotic star. Treating a person well should elicit a certain response, they should reciprocate, they should add to you and then and only then, you should be loyal.

Do you hate your job and your mate? You are an unhappy camper. Never stay in a relationship that is going nowhere fast. If your mate is messing up, start looking for another. There is a lady I know who once stated, "People never change, tell me a person you know of who has changed?" A statement that hurts is usually a true statement that we do not want to be true. She is absolutely correct, bad relationships usually get worse and great relationships last forever.

Great relationships do not require maintenance, you can stay loyal if you are happy, and happiness will keep you together.

II. *Don't*

Just Getting Some Loving

The morning you wake and realize a fling is not your thing.
People who are unhappy may find they are just getting some. Do you have a mate who you are not impressed with? Do you struggle each month to meet your financial obligations? Do you argue more than once a month? If you answered yes to any of these questions, you are just getting some.

Why is this a problem? When this is the issue, every person that walks by looks as if they can fulfil your voids. You can sometimes influence the person you are with to change, however, it is usually time to go. Yes, go, hit the road, start over and break new ground. Persuading a person to do what they are not inclined to do, will certainly build resentment. This is why your mate is called your better half. If there are kids involved this warrants counseling and other energy. If you do not have kids, you should go. Quality people have careers and very little drama. You will have peace of mind and money to enjoy yourself.

Again, your relationship is an investment, invest wisely.

When To Break Up?

Do you keep broken appliances? If your cellphone breaks and you cannot use it, do you keep it because it used to work? No, when things in your life are broken, you get rid of them. If only you could get rid of that relationship that you are not happy with.

Keeping everything may not be the right decision. You cannot get scared in life and keep things that are done serving their purpose. Sometimes keeping a person is a bad idea if you have grown apart. This is not only a book on winning, it is also about which moves to make.

Are you happy? Have you been unhappy for six months? If the answer is yes, you need to go. If you do not go, they will go and you will be alone anyway. If your relationship is ending, go and start something new.

If things are good, you should want to keep your current relationship. If your mate is a good friend of yours, you should stay. Leaving is not the only solution yet sometimes there is nothing left to salvage. You should break it off if you are unhappy. There are many reasons to be unhappy and only you can gauge whether you are unhappy. There are obvious reasons and then there are people who are not compatible. Sometimes there are no arguments, people just do not enjoy their mate's company anymore.

Cut Your Losses

Did you ever want to know how people who invest successfully make millions year after year? Do they have a crystal ball? Is the government behind it? Is it all smoke and mirrors? No, no and no, they understand how to successfully manage their money. This is a combination of getting others to invest and cutting your losses before you lose it all. Hold on, I think you have heard that someplace before. Here, in this book I have told you what works and why.

Finance books are not books full of great stock picks or secrets to great setups. They are full of ways to prepare your mind to trade successfully. I never understood how a strong mind could help you trade, until I started trading. It finally hit me, I am my biggest obstacle. I am the only thing that stands in my way.

Cutting my losses was difficult whenever I traded and it was difficult to do whenever I was involved in a relationship. Once I found you have to lose to win, winning came at a faster pace. The time people spend thinking tentatively is the same time that could be spent winning.

If you could take a look into the future, you would make decisions based on what you know is going to happen. If you knew you were going to need to get another job because your company was downsizing, you would say thank you crystal ball. You would appreciate the tip and start looking for another job. Why not live

Cut Your Losses

your life that way? If you are in a relationship that is not going anyplace, cut it short. You have a look into the future, use those signs to advance. Always look at trends, the trend is your friend. An investor would cut their losses.

Cut your losses and look for the next positive trend.

Troubleshooting

People who are overweight know they are overweight? You have to exercise with them. A person who loves themselves can then and only then love you. Offer to exercise with your mate, if they refuse, you have a big problem. They are not into you, a person who loves you will do anything for you, the same way you will do things for a person you love.

If your favorite star asked you to dye your hair green, you would. People who love each other do not mind doing positive things for each other.

If you want something bad enough, it will happen.

I Am So Into Myself, Why Do People Hate Me?

Who is the proudest person in the room who has done nothing worth boasting about? Who is attached to their phone and does not have a real life? Who is the Weirdo? The social media, web addicted, television watching and I hope they do not date anyone in my family person. If I just described you, take it as a jab, uppercut and body shot. There is a real world out there.

Messaging a person on a social media network does not count as talking to someone. Get out there and do things. If you use social media to set up dates, and get people together to hang out, you are not doing anything wrong. If you spend a great deal of your day commenting on photos and scrolling on your phone, you have a problem.

Studies have shown, social media makes people hate. People hate themselves, they hate others and they hate the world. People release Dope when they are on the verge of getting a reward. There are not any rewards on the social media networks. You are making yourself depressed.

Why are oranges the color orange and bananas are not the color banana? I imagine names can be misleading. There is one thing about social networking, it does not do what is supposed to do by default, make people socialize. People actually become less social the more they socialize on social networks. Social networks make people introverted and appear selfish. People become introverted

I Am So Into Myself, Why Do People Hate Me?

since they rely on the internet to communicate. They become selfish because they imagine talking about themselves will make people like them.

Go out and talk to people. Take one day and do not go on the internet or turn on your television. When you can say hi to the guy at Starbucks, the guy at the pizza place, the lady at the hair salon and your neighbors, you are on your way. You have to love everyone, everyone gets a conversation, listen to everyone and ask questions. Keep smiling.

I am so into myself, why do people hate me, is an idea about how people who are into themselves lose. No one cares about you too much. That is not to say, you are not important, it is just a reminder, in order to receive you must give. Remember, **you have to give in order to take. You can never take without giving. You must give it your all in order to take it all.**

People genuinely care about you if they have an interest in you. If you make a person happy, they will care about you since they care about themselves first and you make them high. If you want a person to like you, start by entertaining them with how beautiful the world is and how great they would become if they took in some of your light.

You will find yourself making lots of friends. You may help them and not get the love in return. People are not evil, they are just selfish. A few disappointments is just a reminder that you have to invest in yourself, just as others have invested in themselves. Do not become selfish, do take time out to walk and maybe put two dollars aside each day to enjoy a massage every three months.

Nobody loves you when you are down and out. People love beauty and when you are doing well, you make them feel great. If you are doing bad, work on doing better, do not talk about doing bad. When was the last time you said, "Come on we should go see John with all the problems, I enjoy hearing him complain?"

I Am So Into Myself, Why Do People Hate Me?

Asking questions is the talking people like, you can count on people to be into themselves, ask them about themselves. Whenever you talk to people about yourself, they listen and they slowly lose interest. They do not care, they do not release Dope and they are not getting addicted. Unless you are a star, no one cares about your life. Ask questions about people when you talk and give your opinion on things, never say anything negative or complain.

Stop loving yourself online, it will only foster bad habits. Talk to people about themselves, you may find out something interesting.

Controller

Want to be miserable? Want to chase your tail like a dog? Want to spend your life trying to figure out what you did wrong? Get into a relationship with a controller. Being nice is one thing, all people should be nice. However, if you find you are the only nice person in the relationship, you are being controlled.

Many people will tell you how they will climb the walls if their favorite heartthrob walked through the door. That is to say, your controller has the potential to love, they just do not feel that way about you. Many people are sitting there saying to themselves, "That is a mean statement." I will reverse the statement, it will become clear. If my favorite star told me they liked a person who enjoyed long walks, I would buy some walking shoes.

Unfortunately, people do things based on value. The sad truth is, when a person allows their value to decrease, people start treating them less valuably. If you find you are being controlled, it is probably too late to do anything about it. Value is a very difficult thing to rebuild. The good news, there are plenty of fish in the sea and some person will treat you well. The grass is greener if your current lawn has died.

People who are being controlled are being walked over. I suggest leaving, I know people and only mean people walk over people. If you are a nice person with a mean person, it will be a battle to change the person's mean ways. Think about it from a mean person's perspective. They can get whatever they want by being mean, what incentive do they have to change? People are nice, they will allow mean people to walk over them and nice people are not confrontational. If you are with a mean, controlling, confrontational person, leaving is far easier than teaching a successful mean person new tricks.

Moving On

Single, just lost the love of your life or just woke up and found you are with a loser. Move on and start moving today. The first thing you need to do, go to new places. Eat lunch where professionals eat, go to malls and go jogging. There are great people out there, you have to be out there to meet them and the club/bar is the worst place to meet your future love.

Get out there and start talking to people. Do not continue to work on your old relationship. Go to some social gatherings and network. Ask some people to introduce you to their friends.

This is a short section, the idea is to take action and get a new life going.

How People Change

Do you love paying the highest price for items at the store? Are you one of those people who take the most difficult route to work? Do you find yourself looking for the longest line at the grocery checkout? If I were to bet, I would bet you answered no to all of those questions. The reason you answered no, people do things that are easy and people only try new things that are easier.

Do you want to sell your phone and buy a model that is more expensive and has less features? No, you would rather keep your current model. Change must be easy, there must be a need and it must be beneficial.

How do we get people to change? We have to sell it to them in a package that is easy, needed and beneficial. The change will take time and persistence. With a little effort, you can positively influence the people around you.

People change when what they are currently doing is harder than the change. What the heck does that mean? People change when it is easier to do something new rather than continue to do what they were already doing. There has to be an incentive to do something new. Sorry, love is not an incentive to change. Love is an incentive to take some punishment that you would not take if you were single. That is bad news but it is the truth. Getting your mate to change could become an eye opener.

How People Change

There has to be a need to have a solution. If a person does not feel there is a need to change, they will not change. Change is the solution if the person imagines they have a problem. You are not going to leave if they do not change. They know this and they do not feel pressured to change. Many people find excuses for being the way they are. The most common excuse, you should love me the way that I am.

How can I make them change? Well, based on what you have learned it has to be easier to do something new. Communicate that you need change and you are going to help them out.

It is possible to want something for a person more than they want it for themselves. Change is not always wanted. Some people wish they could do better and welcome change; others hate it. Remember, **if a person does not feel a need to change, they will not change**. The only way to force change is to increase your value. You can do better yourself or you can leave.

What is value? How do you increase your value? If your mate values you, they will change for you. If your mate were dating a movie star, they would have to do things to please the movie star. The movie star has a high value and it is easier to change and stay with the movie star versus moving back home to an apartment. You have to increase your value to get your mate to cooperate. Many things can be done with words to increase your value. Money does not hurt when it is time to increase your value. Good looks and a bright future will also increase your value.

The key to having a successful relationship: find some person who has the same values as you do. Religious people usually stay together, people who share a culture usually stay together and people on the same page stay together. Telling someone you love they need to lose weight, stop smoking or drinking since it is not healthy should not lead to an argument. Remember, **do not fight to get it right**. If you find yourself at war with your mate, consider ending the relationship.

How People Change

A relationship should add to you. If your partner does not add to you or you have to think of how they add to you, they do not add to you. Getting people to change could become a lifelong battle. It is better to hit the ground running with a person versus changing them while you are in a relationship. Forcing change will lead to resentment and that begets passive aggressive behavior.

Unfortunately, very few people change when there is an addiction involved. People may want to go back to the person they originally were. It is rare to have a person change once there is an addiction.

Drinking and other addictions are very challenging to kick. The best thing to do if you are with a person with addiction issues, set a date and stick to it. Do not make the date more than three months out and have a plan since it is unlikely the person will kick the habit.

Change is an uphill battle. If you find you are unhappy because a person will not change, you can leave or stay unhappy. Not one thing will change if you do not change it. A person is not going to wake up in shape, nice or free of addiction. This all take effort and time. You make yourself happy by putting yourself in happy situations. If you are unhappy, you have no one to blame but yourself. The person who made you unhappy has not sacrificed their happiness for you. They do not care if you are unhappy; why care if they are happy?

Run if a person has issues. It may not sound nice, you are leaving when a person appears to need you most and you imagine you can help. Addiction is an internal struggle and you cannot do anything but love them from a distance. Get them professional help and continue to live your life. Only a professional can help; get help from the experts.

How People Change

I oftentimes tell people to leave. I tell everyone to be positive and many imagine leaving is negative. Change is not negative, people who leave rarely find themselves unhappy in their new relationship. The reason why I tell people to run, I have known people with problems my entire life. Very few, if any have changed. Egos hold people back, people with big egos imagine they can move mountains. People with problems have large egos and do not want to hear about a solution from any person but themselves. It is funny, out of control people imagine they are in control.

Do not imagine you can undo years of depression and addiction with some words or spurts of tough love. **There are very few people who change, do not waste your time or life making a square peg fit into a round hole**. I will tell you what an addict has told me, they do what they want and only they can change themselves.

Live the life you love and love the life you live, that is the purpose of this book. Everyone around you should feel loved. You should light up each room, sidewalk and area. Life is about enjoying. Live, love and laugh.

Remember, **make your next move your best move.**

REMINDERS

INTRODUCTION

Remember, **you have to follow the book to get the results.**

Remember, **the road to success requires you to appear bold; appear bold when you are not feeling bold.**

Remember, **keep going, the worst thing that can happen, will never happen.**

IN THE BEGINNING THERE WAS LIGHT

Remember, **you have to follow the book to get the results.**

Remember, **Socialization Masters are complete people who only add to a setting; they are never in need and avoid those who are in need.**

CREATE OPPORTUNITY

Remember, **procrastinators only hurt themselves.**

WHAT YOUR FRIENDS SAID ABOUT ME

Remember, **keep it positive and make everyone around you laugh and smile.**

VALUE WHAT IS YOUR STORY?

Remember, **if you do not APPEAR to value your look, others will not value it.**

Remember, **your story makes you valuable.**

IS IT IN YOU

Remember, **a business owner who has failed is still a business owner; they have an experience that most will never have.**

Remember, **you have to go to war to enjoy the spoils.**

HOW TO TAKE THE FIRST STEP

Remember, **taking the first step is going to be a sloppy event.**

WHAT IS JEALOUSY?

Remember, **never display negative emotions and never talk about your negative emotions.**

PREPARING YOURSELF

Remember, **if you want to hold onto anything in your past look and not change, put this book down. You do not have what it takes to become a Chief. Every Chief started out as a great Indian.**

Remember, **you sleep with the mind before you sleep with the body.**

REMINDERS

BE POSITIVE

Remember, **only boring people get bored and only negative people have problems.**

GROUPTHINK AND HOW IT RUINED YOUR LIFE

Remember, **there are times when we run from our fears by getting support from those who share the same fears.**

Remember, **always look for guidance from third parties who have no interest in your gains or losses.**

ALL I HAVE TO DO IS BE BETTER THAN YOU, EASY

Remember, **when you feel the competition has outmatched you, do not forget, it is just a feeling.**

THE 1% IS OVERATTED, THE 20% RUN THE WORLD

Remember, **the appearance of something is more important than the truth.**

Remember, **you just need to showcase the 20%.**

Remember, **a difficult situation is an opportunity to lead. If there is chaos or gloom, the leader will be remembered for their courage and ability to lead others toward happiness. Do not fall apart when you are really needed.**

Remember, **the 20% is the wow factor that some people possess and most lack.**

REMINDERS

Remember, **always study people; study the actions of people in real settings, copy what is desirable and avoid what is negative.**

Remember, **most people who are good in social circles are doing it accidentally, they will make mistakes. You are conditioned and you can outshine any person; you are trained to pick up on their mistakes. Make a person's mistakes your strengths.**

Remember **the lion, run faster than your competition and the lion will eat them.**

Remember, **there is something that the most hateful person in the world loves, it is themselves.**

Remember, **people cooperate when they imagine they will benefit from the situation.**

Remember, **people like people who like them.**

Remember, **nothing is real until it is stated and acknowledged.**

BE READY

Remember, **getting the most out of life means sublimating your fear into motivation.**

Remember, **never forget that luck is when preparation meets opportunity.**

CONTRADICTION, NOT WHAT YOU EXPECTED

Remember, **people take the path of least resistance. They will not drum up a complex assessment of you. If you look crazy that is your story; no second chances.**

REMINDERS

SMILE, YOU ARE ON YOUR WAY WITH AN APPETIZER

Remember, **there are two worlds, the mind world and the real world.**

Remember, **a person can make you lose your cool or you can make them keep theirs.**

Remember, **the first thing to go before you blow your cool is your smile.**

MIRROR MIRROR ON THE WALL, THIS PERSON IS DIFFERENT

Remember, **if you get people to agree with you, you are getting them to listen to you.**

Remember, **mirror or be creepy.**

COMMUNICATION

Remember, **the best credential is experience.**

HOW TO BE SOCIAL

Remember, **shyness is just a great fear of rejection.**

NOT COMMUNICATING AND WHAT IT MEANS

Remember, **factual disclosures are less valuable than emotional disclosures.**

Remember, **sharing is caring.**

Remember, **if your mate or friend wants to talk, welcome it and it is a sign of intimacy.**

SAYING NO

Remember, **if you do not stand for something, you will go for anything.**

HOW TO LOOK

Remember, **keep dressing to make yourself happy, you will keep living and socializing alone.**

HOW TO WORKOUT

Remember, **you have to do it to improve it.**

EMOTIONAL CONTAGION, YOUR HAPPINESS IS CONTAGIOUS

Remember, **not making a decision translates into someone making it for you.**

Remember, **understanding lines is not important, understanding minds is important, you can say anything if the person finds you contagious.**

EVERYONE MUST WIN

Remember, **when you are talking to a Potential you are negotiating.**

REMINDERS

CLOSED MOUTHS NEVER GET FED

Remember, **losing is part of winning.**

NETWORKING

Remember, **if at first you do not succeed, ask about their friends.**

YOUNG POTENTIALS

Remember, **people are chasing this person and they have a multitude of people willing to give them things; it is your job to get them to give to you.**

Remember, **an angry person cares and you have made a mark.**

OLDER POTENTIALS

Remember, **do your due diligence, investigate your asset or it could turn into a liability.**

APPROACHING A POTENTIAL WHEN THEY ARE WITH OTHER PEOPLE

Remember, **always ask the power question, "How do you all know each other?"**

PLAYLIST

Remember, **you will win if you pay attention to detail.**

HOW TO KISS

Remember, **you can influence the outcome if you have a great strategy.**

INVESTING

Remember, **they did not invest so they left.**

Remember, **if a person is not giving they are taking.**

Remember, **you want your relationship to be the party where everyone brings a dish.**

I AM SO INTO MYSELF, WHY DO PEOPLE HATE ME

Remember, **you have to give in order to take. You can never take without giving. You must give it your all in order to take it all.**

HOW PEOLE CHANGE

Remember, **if a person does not feel a need to change, they will not change.**

Remember, **do not fight to get it right.**

LIVE, LOVE AND LAUGH

Remember, **make your next move your best move.**

GLOSSARY

Affectional Actions - Action taken as a result of an emotion.

Bounded Rationality - The idea that rationale is subjective. Decisions are made based on the amount of information that a person has. Decisions are satisfying.

Breaking It Down - Looking up the definitions to words to understand what is being communicated. You can then take a large problem and break it into smaller manageable problems.

Build - Constructive actions.

Cognitive Dissonance - Mental discomfort or stress caused by an imbalance, when a person's actions are contradictory to what they are thinking.

Customers - People who get high from a Socialization Master's positive influence. The high makes people enjoy having the Socialization Master around.

Cycle Rule - Repeatedly doing a task so that it becomes natural.

Destroy - Destructive actions including time spent idling, complaining and other negative activities.

Dopamine - A happy pleasurable chemical released by the brain to motivate a person to do certain things.

Dope - Another name for dopamine.

Dove - A very pleasant mate.

GLOSSARY

Duck - A contradiction, aesthetic or verbal inconsistency.

Escape Focus - Focus on a situation as if your life depended on it.

Groupthink - The illusion that everything is okay since your peers are doing it.

Fear Extinction - Removing a fear by being repeatedly exposed to it.

Fly - Aesthetically pleasing, the 20% people are lacking. Purposely doing something to positively stand out.

Halo Effect (HE) - A study that concluded most attractive people are viewed as reliable, smart, trustworthy and kind.

High Self-Monitoring - A person who evaluates the surroundings and adapts to it.

Instrumental Actions - Viewing a person as an object that is used to get what you want.

Investing Game - People are vulnerable when they give. A person who invests will not allow their investment to go bad. If a person invests in you they will not leave you. A person who does not have anything invested has nothing to lose.

Knowledge of Self - Information explaining why people have certain emotions.

Life Satisfaction - The way a person views their present and future life. A very Neurotic individual will view life negatively. Perspective can alter an individual's life more than any physical transformation or economic change.

Low Self-Monitoring - A person who pays no attention to their surroundings and acts based on their emotions.

OCEAN - An acronym used to refer to the five personality traits. It is comprised of Openness, Conscientiousness, Extraversion,

GLOSSARY

Agreeableness and Neuroticism. Openness is a person's capacity for adventure and other experiences. Conscientiousness measures how much self-discipline a person has, not impulsive. Extraversion is a drive to socialize and stimulate others mentally. Agreeableness is the quality that prods people to be positive versus confrontational or negative. Neuroticism is the negative fiber that goads individuals to behave erratically and prefer negative emotions.

Passive aggressive - Anger expressed suggestively.

Procrastinator - An impulsive person who lacks discipline. They have difficulty being productive and will either do nothing or something pleasurable instead of something constructive.

Positivity - A Stoic way of life where negative emotions do not exist. Happiness is the only emotion felt and expressed. Negative emotions are not constructive; they should be avoided.

Potential - A potential mate.

Prognosticating - Talking about one's future in order to make a person appear fly.

Relational Self - Your emotions influenced by your past relationships.

Reward System - The body can make a person crave certain positive behaviors by releasing dopamine. The body makes certain actions pleasurable. Your body gives you a chemical reward and motivates you to laugh, have sex, etc.

Self-Concept - Your introspective, what you think about yourself.

Self-Disclosure - Uncovering a person's self. There are two measures how deep and how much.

Social Exchange - A cost benefit analysis associated with a relationship.

GLOSSARY

Socialization Master (Super) - A person who understands why people have certain emotions.

Start - Take action, do not continue to gain knowledge.

Structural Approach - The idea that the people cooperate when there is a perceived benefit.

Super - Another name for Socialization Master.

War Hawk - A mate who is not pleasant, neurotic.

Winners Circle - Your ideal self.

Work the Room Dance - As soon as you come into the door you talk and shake hands with everyone you see. Man or woman, give them a comment or notice something personal on them. This is done for two reasons: to pleasure yourself and others and to make you popular.

Wounded Deer - A person who shows overt interest in a person without the person doing anything. They will accept any mate; they do not have any standards.

GLOSSARY

Final Gem Confidence

You want to know what confidence is? Confidence is positive thinking; that is all it is, a very simple concept. Whenever you see a person who appears confident they are positive about whatever they are doing. A confident person imagines everything will turn out okay. Actually, the worst thing that could happen will never happen and a confident person is aware of this. Those bad thoughts that paralyze you will never ever happen. It is no magical complex idea that most authors would lead you to believe is unattainable without some fancy direction from them. Yes, you can become confident right now. Have the confidence that most millionaires live with. Start being confident right now by changing the way you view the world. Everyone knows a confident attitude radiates and cannot be faked. People will treat you differently once they see you are confident, a.k.a. positive. Additionally, you will be able to accomplish things such as weight loss, relationship goals, financial objectives and anything you previously struggled with.

Why is confidence important? Why should anyone care about being confident? People have been living their lives for years without being confident, so why rush and become confident now? The answer, becoming confident will make your goals a reality, you will enter the Winner's Circle. When we imagine negative things will happen, guess what? We avoid doing those things that

GLOSSARY

will have a negative outcome. You become fearful and only do things that are safe and routine; there is no growth. Each move we make begins with a thought. Confidence is knowing each move we make will have a positive outcome. With a positive mind we will do the things we dream about. Confidence pushes you to do more

How do we change our negative thinking around? We first look at why it will be easier to be positive. Positive thinking is an addition, it adds to you, your life will be better and easier. You will have more money, better health and great relationships if you are positive and do everything you can to improve your life. First thing we do is change that frown into a smile and only talk about positive things. If a person says it is raining tell them it is a perfect day to read a good book. If you get a flat tire, think of how fortunate you are that it was only a tire and not something more expensive like a dead engine. Second, keep this positive attitude for 100 days, 100 days is what we call the cycle rule. A cycle is used to build a positive habit and positive habits improve our lives. Finally, tell another person about your experience and persuade them do it for 100 days. You have changed your life and you also have a friend who shares and reinforces your beliefs.

Your mind controls your movement, feelings and reality. A powerful mind equates to powerful control over your life. A positive mind is a powerful mind, confident, brave and always focuses on getting up not the fall. Confidence is the key to your success.

www.ingramcontent.com/pod-product-compliance
Lightning Source LLC
Chambersburg PA
CBHW030343240426
43661CB00052B/1724